Tools for the Trenches

TOOLS *for the* TRENCHES

DAILY PRACTICES *for* RESILIENCE, PERSPECTIVE & PROGRESS

ELIZABETH BENTON THOMPSON

TOOLS FOR THE TRENCHES

Daily Practices for Resilience, Perspective & Progress

ISBN 978-1-5445-2479-5 *Hardcover*

978-1-5445-2478-8 *Paperback*

978-1-5445-2477-1 *Ebook*

978-1-5445-2480-1 *Audiobook*

CONTENTS

INTRODUCTION

I started writing this book two weeks after my daughter Dagny died, tragically and unexpectedly. I wrote every word in the darkest, loneliest, and most painful season of my life. I'm fairly certain that the death of a child is the worst thing a human can experience, and we walked that horrific path during an unprecedented global pandemic and quarantine. Funerals (but not liquor stores) were deemed nonessential, support groups stopped meeting, and the pandemic has kept me from seeing most of my local family for over a year. Even as I reflect on it months later, the confluence of impossible circumstances seems more like fiction than reality. Alas, it is my reality.

I've never felt more hopeless, more wounded, or more alone. Trying to survive these circumstances, in a fog of depression and under the weight of post-traumatic stress disorder, has *felt* impossible, but it *isn't* impossible.

I've seen many people emerge from dark times to encourage others, but what I haven't seen as much is people *in* the dark time sharing how they're making it through, moment by moment. **At my own personal bottom, every self-help book felt out of touch and out of reach.** *Tools for the Trenches* is the book I needed but didn't have.

Before experiencing this life-changing loss, I talked and taught about mindset and perspective. More often than not, people struggling with depression, a job loss, or grief would assume that such internal work would have to wait until they were at a better place in their lives. When navigating a hard season in life, so many people disregard these mindset practices in favor of simply getting through the days. They think that working on yourself is a "mountaintop" tool—something reserved for times when life is going smoothly. However, I can tell you with certainty how untrue that is.

Personal tragedy has shown me that becoming a better thinker and adopting new perspectives aren't mountaintop tools; they're tools for the trenches. They matter *most* when life feels hard. They make the biggest impact when you're in the thick of the struggle. These tough times are when it counts.

It doesn't matter if your struggle is small or large. It doesn't matter if it's temporary or permanent. We all need tools to navigate these times in the trenches.

Whether your "trench" is overwhelm, a bad day, the end of a relationship, or a personal tragedy, I want you to know that through these pages, I am with you. I will share my tools, daily practices, and new perspectives with you so that together, we'll emerge stronger.

HOW TO USE THIS BOOK

Let's consider this hypothetical. What if you had consistently implemented and habituated *every* good idea from *every* book you've ever read?

I can't help but smile when I consider that because it's far from my reality!

It almost seems impossible, doesn't it? For most people, at least 95 percent of the tools and ideas they read or hear travel quickly to the idea graveyard—the place where our potential lies dormant under the weight of everything we *could* do *if* we applied ourselves.

I am determined to help you consistently implement the perspectives and practices in the coming pages. I don't want these words to merely inform you. I want them to transform you. I want their impact on your life to extend long after you've turned the last page. I want you to choose to practice implementation and create *new* patterns and responses one moment at a time. That's why the most important thing to remember as you read is: *do not rush.*

When you rush, your highlighted and underlined ideas remain untapped potential, no more valuable than a gift you never opened or a generous check you never cashed.

What does it mean to approach a book as a practice?

Imagine for a second that you're at basketball practice and you hear the coach make suggestions to improve your jump shot. *Square your feet and your hips to the basket. Get a slight bend in your knees. Line up your elbow under the ball. Follow through!*

Hearing those prompts is only step 1A. Your shot won't improve unless you *practice*. You have to put it into action. Outside of that practice session, you'll need to put in time and repetition. You have to work through the steps hundreds or even thousands of times. Knowing *how* to improve your jump shot isn't the same as improving it.

Think of this book in a similar way. When you come across an idea or concept that you want to implement, pause there. Ask yourself, what would it look like for me to make this a practice? What could I do with this today? **Don't confuse information and implementation.** They are universes apart in their look and their impact.

Seek opportunities to practice. You might pick something that you need to practice when you're angry, when you're overwhelmed, or when you're feeling down. Put it in your calendar. Write it in your journal. Carve out time for it today and on future days.

In each chapter, you'll find the "In Practice" section. It's okay to stop there and practice for a while. **Your book doesn't expire.** Take your time and make it count.

Remain committed, less to the turning of the pages and more to practicing the principles that resonate with you and your journey.

Mind the Gap

The mantra I use to keep me mindful of the difference between implementation and information is "*mind the gap.*"

Think of the gap as *the space between what you do and what you know you* could *do if you applied yourself.* What you do includes your habits, choices, behaviors, and perspectives. What you know you *could* do if you applied yourself is comprised of your dreams, hopes, aspirations, goals, and everything you've ever learned in books, courses, and podcasts.

In this day and age where personal development information is everywhere and so easily accessible, there's an unspoken epidemic of people living in the gap.

Our knowledge and understanding of what we *could* do and of what is possible for our lives often grows much faster than our behavior can change.

It produces an uncomfortable gap that most don't even realize they're struggling in.

Your responsibility is to close the gap. Your opportunity is to find ways every day to close the gap by implementing behaviors that embrace your potential and your possibilities, *especially* when life is hard.

Your responsibility goes far beyond learning more and raising your expectations. **You must match that growth with action.** Every day, and every choice made during every day, is a chance to do just that. Every moment and every interaction presents you with an opportunity to show up in a new (maybe better) way.

Shortly after hosting one of my ASCEND weekend workshops, a woman emailed me about a breakthrough she had related to this gap. Here's what she had to say:

"I've been living in the gap and I didn't even know it. That gap has held me back for so long. All of the knowledge and

information I have in my head + the certainty in my bones that I am capable of it all + the inaction...it made me feel like a *crappier* version of myself. Without the action to close the gap, it has just felt like boulders of regret, disappointment, and shame. And those feelings have caused me to miss out on so. freaking. much.

I know now that regret/shame/disappointment are just the gap. Every choice I make either widens the gap or closes the gap. Even the smallest great choice lessens the tension and closes the gap.

*That realization alone—that **those awful feelings are just a signal that I'm in the gap**—takes ALL of the power away from those feelings. And it's so easy to break through it. It doesn't take a Herculean effort. Just one step to close it a little."*

If you've ever felt like a failure, like a fraud, or like you lack the discipline to do the things you want or need to do, those feelings are less a reflection of you and more a reflection of where you are: in the gap. **Those feelings are evidence of *where* you are, not *who* you are.**

One of my very favorite quotes that speaks to this gap comes from author and poet Mark Nepo.

*"To always analyze and problem solve and observe and criticize what we encounter turns our brains into heavy calluses. Rather than opening us deeper into the mystery of living, **the***

overtrained intellect becomes a buffer from experience." (Emphasis mine)

The overtrained intellect becomes a buffer from experience.

Can you relate to that? I'm here to break that pattern with you.

When we take action, we downshift the thinking brain so we can throttle experience.

We're here to improve the balance between learning and doing—these need to move in tandem.

You don't have to intellectualize self-improvement. You need to *implement* it. Experience teaches you in a way that knowledge can't.

It's not enough to know the gap exists or even identify that you're in it. **We must choose our way out of it, one moment of opportunity at a time.**

As you move through these pages, be mindful of the gap and come back, over and over, to implementation.

PROLOGUE

My world changed in June of 2019. What started as the most thrilling and heart-expanding time of life ended in a tragedy that I wasn't sure I would survive.

It all started when I found out we were pregnant! Chris and I had decided we were ready to start a family but never imagined we would conceive the very first month we started trying.

Overall, my pregnancy was unremarkable. I was healthy, my baby girl was healthy, and my only consistent complaint was insomnia. A friend of ours commented that she had never seen a woman rub or rock her pregnant belly more than I did mine.

My February 29 due date came and went, and, like most full-term moms, I was *more* than ready to meet our daughter!

On March 4, 2020, I woke my husband, Chris, around 7

a.m. I hadn't slept (again), and on this particular morning I was starting to feel sick. I figured it was my body preparing for delivery, but we decided to call the doctor just in case there was cause for concern. I had a very low-grade fever, but it was enough for the doctor to suggest that we come in so they could monitor me for an hour. While we were there, they'd give me an oral medication to help soften my cervix.

Shortly after getting checked in, they let us know that we *wouldn't* be heading home after an hour; due to my fever, we were there until baby girl arrived. They gave me some Tylenol, which brought my fever down, and told me they'd keep an eye on it.

The day was uneventful; I worked on my laptop and took walks through the hospital halls with Chris. The Tylenol seemed to be keeping the fever down, so we settled in to wait for labor to progress.

The following afternoon, my water broke and my contractions felt pretty manageable. Around 8 p.m., my fever spiked again, and the doctor suggested I stop eating and drinking just in case there was a C-section in my future. Meanwhile, the frequency and intensity of my contractions started to pick up. I played the Jai-Jagdeesh version of "Hallelujah" on repeat while Chris counted down each contraction.

By 11:30 p.m., I was exhausted but couldn't sleep through the discomfort of contractions. My doctor gave me a small dose of morphine so I could get some rest before the action started. I hadn't slept in two days, and it was showing.

After a couple of hours of much-needed sleep, I woke to still stronger contractions but was only about four centimeters dilated. My nurse came in to check my temperature and it was over 104 degrees—dangerously high for both me and baby. From there, everything became pretty urgent.

My doctor, freshly awoken from the call room, let me know that we were going to the operating room for an emergency C-section. Baby was fine, but my fever was alarming. They thought it might be a sign of a bacterial infection called chorioamnionitis, which occurs before or during labor and could put our daughter at risk.

I was terrified. Throughout my pregnancy, I never considered a C-section. Now, here we raced to sign consent forms and start new IVs. With tears streaming down my frightened face, I listened to the doctor go over the risks while Chris texted our parents with the update.

I remember asking the anesthesiologist, with great concern, if he was awake enough to care for me well. After all, it was about 3 a.m. (I don't think my question even registered with him, to be honest.)

As they pushed my hospital bed to the operating room, I called for Chris. Urgently I told him, *"Her name is Dagny, okay?"* We had been waiting to meet her before finalizing her name but in that moment, I knew. *"Her name is Dagny because she's strong. She's a fighter."*

An avid reader, one of my all-time favorite books is Ayn Rand's classic *Atlas Shrugged*. The lead female in the book is named Dagny. I'm sure you'll understand why we chose that name when you read how the literary community has described her character.

"Dagny is remarkable in every way: beautiful, talented, determined, and highly intelligent. Her independent spirit leads her to trust her own judgment over public opinion. Though calmly rational, she is also tremendously passionate about her work and love. She is enormously successful as a woman in a man's world. Rand presents her this way to demonstrate that rationality and great accomplishments are not gender-specific." (SparkNotes)

Once in the operating room, I received my epidural and immediately started shaking. The shaking was so intense that I was struggling to breathe. Frantically, I begged Chris for help. He held my hand, modeling each inhale and exhale, until after what felt like hours but was surely only minutes, we heard a tiny but determined shout of arrival.

Our sweet girl was here! She didn't cry, but she did give us a clear exclamation of her entrance into the world.

Chris followed as they carried her to the corner of the room. I kept asking, *"Is she okay? Is everything okay? Chris! Can you see her? Is she okay?"*

She was more than okay—beautiful, healthy, and strong. Dagny was born on Friday, March 6 at 4:31 a.m. She was a perfect seven pounds, ten ounces.

Chris carried her over and held her to my face. The very first thing she did was lick my cheek. For as long as I live, I won't forget that moment.

The next few days were pretty uneventful. My fever broke within minutes of delivery. The doctors ran a battery of tests to figure out the cause of my fever and reduce Dagny's likelihood of infection before or during birth. They sent my placenta to be biopsied and eventually ruled out chorioamnionitis and any bacterial infection. After extensive testing, they figured the fever was just a fluke and we were both alright.

Tired but happy, we brought Dagny home. At home, nursing was a struggle. Getting Dagny to latch was a team effort, but we were so in love with her that we soaked up every moment of troubleshooting. We had been told that the first two weeks of breastfeeding are the hardest, so we kept at it.

Dagny's first pediatrician appointments were normal and healthy. She wasn't yet back to her birth weight, but again, we felt (and were told repeatedly) this was normal, especially for a breastfed baby. I started pumping to see if we might have better luck with longer feedings from a bottle. Plus, this allowed Chris to do the 2 a.m. or 3 a.m. feedings, so I could get a couple of hours of sleep.

Early Wednesday morning, March 18, she didn't want to take her bottle. Chris woke me up to nurse her, but she wasn't interested in that either. Fortunately, we had a regularly scheduled pediatrician appointment later that morning and planned to talk about it then. She still had regular diapers, and it was just that one feeding, so we remained unconcerned.

The pediatrician wasn't concerned either. He suggested we come back to check on her weight on Monday. I felt like that was a little too long, so we agreed to come back on Friday instead.

On our drive home, the pediatrician called. He said, *"On second thought, I want to make sure she doesn't get dehydrated. That can happen quickly in newborns; when you get home, pump and see if she will take two and a half ounces. If she doesn't, take her to your nearest pediatric emergency room because she might need fluids. If she is even a little dehydrated, she might lose interest in eating, so fluids can solve the problem quickly."*

Once home, I pumped a few ounces, and she drank two. Now, we had to decide whether to drive an hour (during the coronavirus pandemic) and take her to an ER or count two ounces as "pretty good" and return to the pediatrician in the morning.

We debated. We hemmed and hawed. Dagny didn't look sick. She had frequent wet diapers but wasn't fussy. Eventually, we decided to err on the side of caution and packed her in the car for the hour trip to our nearest pediatric emergency room.

We had no idea that we would never bring her home.

At the ER, doctors and nurses immediately reassured us. They told us she was likely mildly dehydrated, so they started her on IV fluids. *"We're going to top her off and you'll be home in a few hours!"*

I hated seeing her with an IV, but I believed the doctors. She didn't have a fever; she wasn't listless. In fact, the nurses commented on how feisty she was. While I pumped in the corner of the room, she aggressively sucked sugar water off Chris's finger.

They wanted to bring us up to a pediatrics room while she got her fluids, where Chris and I would both have a place to lie down. Only a few hours later, Dagny started to struggle. She kept making this odd coughing noise, and every few minutes I'd ask the nurse, *"Is that normal? She's never made that sound before."* After nagging the nurse repeatedly, they brought Dagny down for an X-ray. Minutes later, they told us it appeared that Dagny had a bowel obstruction, and we needed to go to Boston Children's Hospital by ambulance for emergency surgery.

Suddenly, the dark, quiet room filled with people and a frantic, frightening energy. Through tears, I said to no one in particular, *"She's going to be okay, right?"* The only answer I expected was, *"Of course!"* but that's not what I heard.

Without taking his eyes off Dagny, the neonatologist gravely replied, *"She's very, very sick."*

She's very, very sick? What the hell do you mean? She was just mildly dehydrated and they were topping her off with fluids and we were going right home!

It seemed to take forever for them to prep her for transport to Boston. I later learned that it took so long because she was dying. They struggled to stabilize her. All her vitals crashed. Her heart failed.

Chris and I stood in the corner of the room looking on with disbelief and pure horror. Still, in our minds, we thought we'd have our sweet newborn in abdominal surgery, they'd clear the blockage, and we'd have a slow road to recovery.

We would soon learn there was no blockage and there would be no recovery.

It was a cold, rainy morning as I climbed into the front seat of the ambulance and they loaded Dagny into the back. Chris followed behind in our car. Because of COVID, there was very little traffic, even into Boston during rush hour—a minor miracle. Had there been typical traffic, Dagny would have died before we arrived.

Our ambulance driver was a kind, gentle man named Joe. Joe told me that Boston Children's Hospital is the best in the world, and we wanted to get Dagny the best care possible. He told me this would be a long road. We would be in Boston for a long time and come to know these roads well. We'd come to know the doctors and nurses well, too.

I remember him saying, *"If they can save her, this will be a long road for your family."*

If?! We were just home with her. She was just fine.

We raced to Boston. Joe told me that when we arrived, things would move very quickly. The hospital called on the radio to get my consent for surgery so she could go right to the operating room. There wouldn't even be time for me to sign papers or speak to her surgeon.

As we pulled up to the hospital's ambulance bay, the team was already outside, waiting for us in the rain. I was barely out of my seat and they had her unloaded and were racing through the doors. I couldn't kiss her, touch her hand, or say goodbye.

A woman came to greet me and brought me to a waiting room. I had just sat down when Joe threw the door open.

"Mom. We need Mom. We're losing her, and you need to say goodbye."

Oh my God. What? Chris isn't here yet! Say goodbye?

Joe took my hand, and we ran down the hall. I wasn't yet two weeks post-C-section. My incision stretched painfully with each hurried step, but I didn't care.

Without pausing for the precaution of scrubs or a mask, they rushed me into the operating room. At least a dozen people filled the huge room. They pulled forward a tall, silver chair with white cushions and helped me into it.

I was bewildered as I observed their collective urgency.

After a terrifying minute, a nurse looked at me and calmly said to no one in particular, *"What is she doing in here? She can't be in here. Get her out!"*

Without words, three nurses escorted me back to the waiting room. On the way, Chris burst through the Emergency Department door. He knew by my face that something was very, very wrong.

I burst into hysterical tears and stammered, *"They told me she's dying! They brought me into the operating room to say goodbye!"*

Stunned, Chris said nothing.

We numbly followed these strangers back towards the private waiting room, but before we got to the door, it happened *again*.

Someone ran up to us in the hall and said, *"We need mom and dad! You need to say goodbye."* We ran back to the doors of the same operating room, but someone stopped us at the door. I'll never forget watching Chris's legs collapse beneath him as he processed what was happening.

"What are you doing to these poor people? You can't keep bring-

ing them back and forth. They need to sit down. They can't go in."

We never went back in. We were escorted back to that small waiting room and informed that they would send us a chaplain.

A chaplain. I understood the meaning of that.

What the hell was happening? How did this happen? What's going on? What's wrong with my baby? I texted my mom and told her to hurry.

I'm pretty sure it was hours before the surgeon finally came in to speak to us. He was a tall, middle-aged man who didn't look like he had good news to share. I wish I could remember everything he said, but essentially, he told us that she was still alive, though barely.

Her heart stopped upon arriving at the hospital, before they could get her to the operating room. She received chest compressions for thirty minutes before they could successfully get her on heart-lung bypass (ECMO). Surgery had revealed that there was no bowel obstruction. They could not close her abdominal incision due to the tremendous swelling of her liver and spleen that happened with rapid onset. There was a plastic dome over her belly to protect it. In the absence of a bowel obstruction, they didn't know why she was so sick but hoped ECMO would buy enough time to see if she could recover.

It didn't look good.

They told us to wait a while longer until they got her up to the neonatal intensive care unit, and then we could see her. When they finally invited us back to see her, I was terrified. The doctors warned us she didn't look like herself. They encouraged us to prepare ourselves for a difficult sight, but I didn't know how to make those preparations.

Chris and I walked back, desperate to be with her, speechless in our pain. I will spare you the descriptions, but nothing could have prepared me to see her like that. If they hadn't told us that was our Dagny, I wouldn't have believed it.

For hours, we stood by her side, unable to hold her. I cried and begged for God to save her. I sobbed. I wailed. I sang to her. I touched her tiny, swollen, cold hands. I prayed over her. I talked to her about the life we wanted for her and our little family.

Meanwhile, while all this was happening, I thought I was having a stroke, I was bleeding so heavily from my C-section recovery. I had seen all the warning signs. My blood pressure shot through the roof, I had a migraine, and I passed blood clots larger than golf balls. In hindsight, we're pretty sure I was suffering from eclampsia. Of course, I didn't care one bit about any of that. The only thing that mattered was Dagny.

I vividly remember one moment, looking at Dagny from a distance while a team of doctors and nurses cared for her and asking with obvious desperation, *"Can someone give me some good news?"* I think I expected to hear that she would pull through or that she had started showing signs of improvement.

Deafening silence answered my question.

Eventually, someone said, *"Well, they were able to get her on bypass."*

I knew it was bad, but I was sure in my heart that she would be our miracle baby and would somehow pull through this. I was certain. I felt a knowing in my heart that God would get her through this.

A few hours later, we ran into her surgeon in the cafeteria. He recognized us immediately and stopped to give us an update. I vividly remember him saying, *"We still have to thread the eye of the needle."* He hoped she'd show some signs of improvement overnight.

We checked into a hotel next to the hospital so I could pump and we could shower. As I set up the breast pump, Chris tried to encourage me. *"She's going to need your milk to get stronger. There's a long recovery ahead."*

Early the next morning, after pumping again, we walked back to the hospital. As parents of a baby in the NICU, you have an access card to get back there any time, day or night. The day before, they had explained this and told us that they would never deny us access to Dagny. Yet, when we passed the desk to go to her, the attendant told us to stay in the waiting room.

I was immediately alarmed. Chris thought that maybe they were doing rounds or a bedside procedure and that's why they asked us to wait. As I panicked, he kept telling me that everything was fine. If it wasn't, he reasoned, they would have called us.

Everything wasn't fine.

Twenty minutes later, the surgeon and the neonatologist came out to the waiting room. I have no recollection of what they said except that we needed to say our goodbyes and call our family priest if we wanted to have her baptized before she died.

They still had no idea what was wrong with her, but she wasn't going to make it. A bypass machine mechanically kept her alive. They explained that at this point, a diagnosis would only be possible after an autopsy, and someone would talk to us soon about those options.

We stared at them.

We just stared at them.

What are you supposed to say?

The rest of the morning was a living nightmare. The moments are still too painful for words. That morning is carved into my consciousness, those hours where we said goodbye to our daughter while begging for an unlikely miracle. We gathered what family we could. We had impossible conversations about where they would take her body once they disconnected her from machines, about autopsies. Chris held her while a priest baptized her, our tears soaking her white dress.

I kissed her cold head, and we left the room, leaving our dreams, our hearts, and our daughter in that NICU room.

We left the hospital with just a parking pass.

Dagny's battle for survival ended that day, and mine was just beginning.

The coming pages are about surviving life's challenges and finding ways to be your own best asset and biggest ally, even when you don't think you can.

I hope you find these tools and strategies as valuable as they continue to be for me.

THE COURAGE
OF THE SEED

In July of 2019, we hosted a party to announce our pregnancy with Dagny. I was only about six weeks pregnant, but we decided to share the news early. I would soon travel to California to celebrate my birthday and Primal Potential's five-year anniversary at a tequila-themed celebration, where I assumed people would grow suspicious as I declined to drink. As we prepared for our party, Chris took a table from the basement and set it outside for food and drinks. After the party, I'm pretty sure I asked him *at least* once a month to put the table back in the basement. In April 2020, ten months after the party and one month after Dagny's death, the table was *still* outside, leaned against a stone wall beside our deck.

In a moment of obvious overwhelm and frustration, I asked Chris, *"How is it that you have time to do the things you want to do? You have the time to help other people, but I've been asking you to put that table back in the basement—a task that will take you less than five minutes—for almost a year, and you've yet to follow through? Move the table today!"*

By some miracle, he did it. It took just three minutes, and the old table was finally back in the basement and no longer sitting out in our yard. I came out of my office and instead of being faced with the grimy tabletop, I could see our stone wall and the spring's mud around it.

But there was something else. It wasn't just the rock and mud I was expecting to see. Something surprising immediately caught my eye. Against the rocks, where the table had been for ten months, in an area that had received no sunlight for nearly a year, was one singular purple hyacinth.

I have no idea how it managed to push through the mud and the rocks without the aid of sunlight, but it did. As I was writing this, I went back to find the picture I took of this lone flower, only to find that I had discovered it on April 20, exactly one month from the day Dagny died.

In a way, I was grateful Chris hadn't moved the table (though I don't plan to tell *him* that) because seeing that unlikely flower made an impression on me.

Somehow, life finds a way to break through. Even when there's no light, even when the odds are against you and it seems utterly impossible, there's still a way to break through and bloom.

In *The Book of Awakening*, Mark Nepo tells a similar story, and it continues to bring me hope and comfort.

"All the buried seeds

crack open in the dark

the instant they surrender

to a process they can't see

*All around us, everything small and buried surrenders **to a process that none of the buried parts can see**. And this innate surrender allows everything edible and fragrant to **break ground into a life of light** that we call spring.*

*In nature, we are quietly given countless models of **how to give ourselves over to what appears dark and hopeless**, but which ultimately is **an awakening that is beyond all imagining**. This moving through the dark into blossom is the threshold to God.*

*As a seed buried in the earth cannot imagine itself as an orchid or hyacinth, **neither can a heart packed with hurt imagine itself loved or at peace**. The courage of the seed is that once cracking, it cracks all the way."* (Emphasis mine)

I've read that passage at least one thousand times since Dagny died. We won't see it. We can't force it. We don't even influence it. And still, it happens: light, spring, change, breakthrough, healing. None of the buried parts can see it. Yet, there is a model for giving ourselves over to what appears dark and hopeless, but isn't.

Dagny died on March 20 when everything was still dark and lifeless. In the coming weeks, dark and lifeless completed its predictable and beautiful about-face.

Warmth followed cold.

Sun followed rain.

Life followed death.

It's everywhere, and yet, despite all this perennial evidence, we don't always believe our lives will cycle in similar patterns.

In my personal winter, everything seemed cold, dark, and hopeless. Whether I wanted to acknowledge it or not, nature reminded me that there are no unending seasons.

One day shortly after Dagny died, I was walking along the canal by our home, thinking of the beautiful white afghan blanket my then ninety-five-year-old grandmother made for

Dagny. It covered her car seat the day we brought her to the emergency room, unaware she would never occupy it again. My grandmother told me it was the last afghan she would ever make due to her worsening arthritis. I realized that when starting a project like that—a handmade afghan or any number of the impeccable quilts that were made for Dagny— *at some point, it looks more like a mess than a masterpiece.*

But a mess *isn't* a mess; it's a stage in an unfinished process. It's a piece of something much bigger, something we can't yet see.

I reminded myself that we shouldn't equate the early stages to the final product. Often, we can't even *imagine* what it might become. Weeks after losing Dagny, I thought my life was over. I thought I'd never laugh again. I didn't think I could survive the pain, and I didn't want to. I couldn't conceive of any type of masterpiece.

Like Dagny's afghan, trial is a process. We must allow it to unfold, to come together with a thread called vision and a needle called time. Throughout our lives, we craft something we can't yet see with threads of patience and steadfastness.

The courage of the seed—it cracks open in the dark. It blooms through a process it can't see. It blooms through a process many of us can't see. But it blooms.

We can't see the process.

We might not understand the process.

We might not even trust the process.

It happens anyway.

New love follows heartbreak.

Hope follows despair.

Life follows loss.

What appears to be a mess is just one stage in an unfinished process. What appears to be a mess might actually be the development of a masterpiece—something bigger than we can yet see or even imagine.

In Practice:

Sometimes, we have to begin by convincing ourselves that change is true and possible. Where can you find evidence for things happening that you don't see? Is there evidence in your home? In your past? In your yard?

What do you need to change about your thoughts to change your beliefs?

What do you need to change about your thoughts to stay mindful.

What do you need to change about your thoughts to remain inspired?

Where in life have you seen love follow heartbreak? Do you know someone who has found love after loss? Who's gotten a better opportunity after losing one? Have you ever or do you know someone who has created or experienced success after a setback?

FRUITFUL

In the summer of 2018, while living in my newly custom-built tiny house, I decided to buy an investment property in New Hampshire. I had paid cash for the tiny house and my expenses were low, so it seemed to be an ideal time to invest in other real estate.

A couple of months after purchasing my New Hampshire investment property, though entirely *not* in the market to buy again, I suggested to Chris that we drive around and look at houses in our area. We both love real estate, and it is always a great way for me to mentally disconnect from work and life stress.

We came across a major fixer-upper with a ton of potential in an incredible location, just a stone's throw from the water. It had hit the market that very day, and we impulsively made an offer. We thought it would be a fun, fairly low-risk project we could use as our first flip.

Because it was a new listing, the seller decided not to respond to our offer for five days to see what other kinds of bids they might get. On the third day, Chris and I once again went for a drive to check out homes for sale and spotted a small, hardly noticeable sign in front of a charming but *very* old house. I wasn't sure if it was a construction sign, a historical sign, or a for sale sign. We drove by one more time and sure enough, it was a for sale sign. This historic home sat on a multi-acre lot that appeared to have a thirty- or forty-tree apple orchard on it!

I asked Chris, who's a real estate agent, *"Can you get us in there? I just want to see it."*

Because I grew up in a colonial New England home, I feel nostalgic for the charm and history of old homes. Chris and I looked this one up online and found it was built in 1707! While I wasn't looking to move out of my tiny house and we had an over-ask offer in on *another* house just a few miles away, I was curious to check it out.

The next morning, we walked through the house. It was dark and dated, but I could see a ton of potential. A little bitter over the fact that the owners of the other property weren't responding to our generous offer, we decided to put in an offer on *this* one.

The sellers countered quickly, and we accepted their

counter. When the owners of the other house reached out the following day to accept our offer, we let them know that, unfortunately, we had decided to move in another direction. What a turn of events. We were about to purchase a massive project with a ton of potential and I guess move in together!

Once we moved in, one of the first things we needed to do was prune the apple orchard. It had been at least ten years since the property was last cared for with any regularity, and the trees were seriously overgrown. The limbs had grown together into a tangled canopy, blocking essential light.

Chris's uncle, who has some experience with such things, came by every day for weeks to spearhead the project. As he pruned the trees, it looked more like destruction than caretaking.

I had never done anything like this before. I wasn't sure if we were saving the trees or killing them. Apparently, others also had their doubts. Several concerned locals came right up to our door and spouted angry inquiries:

"Why are you cutting down the apple trees?"

"The prior owners would be devastated that you're destroying this orchard!"

"You need to stop! You can't destroy this property!"

Chris assured them that we weren't destroying it, we were merely pruning it. We were making it better, healthier, and stronger. However, we both wondered what would happen when the weather turned. Would the trees blossom and produce fruit? Had we gone too far?

Sure enough, when spring came, the trees responded enthusiastically. New branches began to shoot up. Each tree had well over one hundred new baby branches. Thousands of apple blossoms celebrated their access to the sun.

We continue to prune the trees—it's an ongoing process— always nervous that the trees won't respond, and yet, every single time, new life replaces what we cut away.

You'd think that would be some big, powerful lesson in my life, but just a few months after seeing the regrowth of the apple trees, I was back to doubting the whole process, this time with my beloved lilacs.

Lilacs are my favorite flower, and we have huge groves of lilac trees scattered about our property. When a friend told us they, too, were overgrown and needed to be dramatically cut back, I didn't want him to do it. Trusting his expertise, I reluctantly agreed and watched in horror as he pruned my lilac trees. *"I'm going to be so upset if they don't come back,"* I told Chris.

Sure enough, they not only came back, they came back

with noticeably more flowers. They didn't just flower again, but the pruning allowed for a multitude of new growth, far greater than what we had just one year before.

Without the pruning, both the apple trees and the lilacs would have eventually died.

After Dagny died, I was sitting with my Bible and stopped for some much-needed contemplation when I turned to John 15:1–2.

*"I am the vine and my Father is the gardener. He cuts off every branch in me that bears no fruit, while **every branch that does bear fruit he prunes so that it will be even more fruitful.**"* (Emphasis mine)

...so that it will be even more fruitful.

Pruning is not a punishment. Though pruning can feel and even *look* like loss, *pruning doesn't take away.* Pruning makes us more fruitful. It is *required* for new growth and better production so that we might have even greater abundance.

I'm not here to suggest that Dagny was intentionally removed from my life, by God or anything else. The reality is, I will not know in this lifetime why she died. However, I *do* see that though I don't feel it and though it doesn't *look* like it, this tragedy could bring even more life into my life. It could result in bearing even more fruit.

The combination of COVID-19 and Dagny's death (happening synchronously) pruned a lot of people from our lives. The pruning of relationships added a whole other layer of grief, the last thing I felt I needed while mourning the agonizing death of our daughter. Our world seemed to get so much smaller.

It took me many months to see this perspective, but I see it more and more each day now: maybe what was happening in our relationships wasn't loss at all but pruning. What was removed was replaced by deeper, richer relationships. More often than not, what once looked and felt like a void actually created room for abundance not otherwise possible.

Loss is always fruitful. You might not initially see it or ever acknowledge it. It's okay if you don't welcome it. But it is fruitful.

In my first book, *Chasing Cupcakes,* I wrote about my strained relationship with my mom because of the way she "addressed" my weight in our home. Our relationship was fully restored and strengthened in ways I couldn't have imagined after the loss of Dagny. I saw a maternal side of my mom that I haven't ever seen, in her bravery while Dagny lay dying and in her steadfastness in the weeks and months after Dagny's death.

I also know that the experience of losing Dagny and then going through the grieving process without the support we expected has transformed and multiplied the vision we have for our family. We will have a larger family—a closer family—because of this experience. We will show up for others differently. This experience has uniquely bonded us.

When we arrived at the church for Dagny's funeral, there was a ring of cars around the outer perimeter of the parking lot. It almost looked like there was an event at the school across the street, but because of COVID I knew that wasn't the case. As we got closer, I saw people standing outside their cars. *"They're singing,"* I said to Chris.

My mom's friends, most of whom didn't know me, all of whom didn't know Chris or Dagny, had shown up at the church with posters expressing love and support, and they were singing to us. They did not expect entry into the church because of the pandemic, but they showed up anyway. Some of them had driven hours to be there. Thinking about it still makes me cry.

As we left the church over an hour later, we saw even more cars. People had stayed, and more had come. My mom's friends still sang to show their support.

The day Dagny died, Chris and I decided to start a foundation in her name to support other families who are navigating infant crisis and loss. It's yet another example of fruitfulness. It's an impact we wouldn't have made without our loss.

I'll be honest—I'd rather have Dagny here than have the impact of her foundation. I'd rather have Dagny here than have a clearer vision for our family. However, I don't get to make that choice, just like my apples and lilacs didn't have a choice in their pruning.

Yes, it crushes my heart to entertain the possibility that an abundance of good could come from Dagny's death. It's a gross understatement to say the mere notion hurts. I hate it. I don't want it. I wish I could have it another way.

Here's the thing, though: the way pruning works holds true whether we like it or not, whether we opt for it or not. It exists to bring more life, more growth, and more fruitfulness, not less.

Even though you don't like it, want it, or get it, it's still true.

You can hate gravity, but its laws still apply in your life.

Pruning is painful but essential, too. Its results are beautiful.

The pruning in your life could be the loss of a friendship, a job, an opportunity, or even a loved one.

It's okay that it feels like loss. It *is* loss. It's okay to be afraid. It's okay that you aren't sure if new life will spring forth or if you ache in the wake of pruning. It's that needle called time. Allow for the work of time and remain open to the possibility that more fruit will be borne because of this loss.

Pruning doesn't take place to take *away*; it happens so that we might have more, so that we might be twice as fruitful.

In the two years we've lived on our growing hobby farm, we've learned that there are right ways and wrong ways to prune. For example, you don't want to prune the limbs that grow out; you want to prune the limbs that grow down. You don't want to prune in the warm months but cold months. The instrument you use to prune could be a weapon of destruction or a tool to multiply growth. It just depends on *how* you use it.

The same is true of the tools we use in our lives. Whether we're talking about food, spending, communication, social media, or anything in between, these things can help us grow or cause us harm, depending on how and when we use them.

I regularly ask myself, *"Does this support me or does this harm me? Does this assist in my healing or does this impair my healing? Am I using this in a way that helps or hurts?"*

Sometimes, I'm evaluating a food choice. Does this choice heal my body and mind, or am I using it to escape?

Sleeping and rest can be powerful tools or dangerous weapons, depending on how we use them. There have been days when I don't want to get out of bed. On those days, I have to ask myself: Am I using rest as a tool right now? Am I using it as a weapon?

I take the same line of inquiry when I'm replaying every second of Dagny's life, every decision we made and every conversation with doctors. Am I using reflection as a tool to help me heal? Or, in this moment, am I using it as a weapon to prevent my healing? Sometimes, the reflection is beautiful and memorializing. Sometimes, the reflection is instructive and peace-giving. It's helpful to know that we might do something different with future pregnancies, deliveries, or newborns. Other times, it's unproductive and damaging.

Sometimes, I'm reflecting on things that were said or not said, done or not done in a way that is objective and helps me gain clarity on what I want for our life and our family and our friendships. Other times, it's a fixation that only serves to make me want to isolate. It fosters an anger that I don't want to have or feel.

In life, we often want things to be black or white. We

want reflection to either be helpful or harmful. We want anger to either be good or bad. Realistically, it's almost always both.

It depends on how you're using it, and it's up to you to pay attention.

In Practice:

Ask yourself, *Do I believe in pruning?* What is your definition of pruning? Where have you seen that definition ring true in your own life or your understanding of life in general?

Where has loss created abundance?

How do you need to think to believe in this concept?

How do you need to think to remain inspired by it?

Is there a place where it feels possible for you to shift from a perspective of loss to a perspective of pruning and impending fruitfulness?

Where might you be using something as a weapon that you would feel much better using as a tool?

Start evaluating your thoughts, decisions, choices, and

behaviors. Ask yourself, *"Am I using this as a weapon or a tool?"*

You might even ask, *"What makes this a tool?"* or *"What makes this a weapon?"*

Look at your communication style: are you using it as a weapon or a tool?

What would it look like to use communication as a tool today?

What would it look like to use communication as a weapon today?

What would it look like to use food as a tool today?

What would it look like to use food as a weapon today?

What would it look like to use media (social/news/TV) as a tool today?

What would it look like to use media (social/news/TV) as a weapon today?

IT'S NOT PRETTY, BUT IT WILL BE PRODUCTIVE

Devastation. A city after a bomb has ravaged it. A floor covered in wooden blocks after a child has knocked all the "buildings" down.

That's what my life felt like—what it *looked* like—in the weeks after Dagny died.

Though it pales in comparison, it wasn't just the sudden and horrific death of our daughter. COVID-19 had just hit in full force...during the middle of a product launch for Primal Potential that should have represented nearly a quarter of our annual revenue. The devastation wasn't limited to my personal life.

The day after Dagny died, we got a call from the hospital where she was born. Due to a clerical issue with her birth certificate, they said, we'd have to return to the hospital to sign a new one before they could issue a death certificate. They wouldn't release her body to the funeral home until that happened.

While we drove to the hospital, I had a call with Primal Potential's COO. Normally, we'd never have a work call during such a personal crisis, except the business was in a crisis of its own.

"The launch isn't going well," Suzie told me. We weren't even at 5 percent of where we expected to be. Businesses were shutting down, quarantine and mandatory closures had just started, and in the uncertainty, people didn't want to spend money.

She suggested we cancel the launch altogether, eliminating a minimum of several hundred thousand dollars' worth of revenue. It wasn't just the lost launch revenue; we had spent tens of thousands gearing up for this launch.

Forty-eight hours after losing my daughter, I numbly confronted serious business issues that I couldn't ignore. *"Is this even real?"* I wondered. We had salaries to pay and families to take care of. Chris and I were facing a mountain of medical bills and funeral expenses.

We had no idea how long the financial impact of the shutdown would last. Everything seemed so dark.

To make matters worse (as unfathomable as that may seem), the state in which we live had just declared funerals nonessential. At two weeks postpartum, I didn't have any clothes that fit and would be suitable for my daughter's funeral, but all the stores were closed. It felt apocalyptic.

We started to plan for an out-of-state funeral but received daily updates that the governor there would soon follow suit and ban funerals.

I sat in the car, breasts full of milk, aching physically, about to re-sign the *birth* certificate for my now deceased child, my livelihood feeling threatened by the financial toll of COVID-19...it felt like a massive bomb had detonated in my life.

As much as I didn't want to consider this perspective, I knew there was factual truth in this:

Devastation is an opportunity for rebuilding.

As kids, we loved to make forts. Sometimes we made them out in the woods under trees; sometimes, in the living room. One time, we made an epic fort right against the back of the house. My stepdad, a contractor, had an endless supply of scrap materials for us to use. This particular fort was special. For some reason, I remember it being better than all the rest. We left it up for at least a week, holding meetings in it, having snacks, playing games, and bringing books out to read in the seclusion of our imaginative creation. Then, believing we could do better, we destroyed it. With its destruction came the opportunity to rebuild. These work in tandem.

If COVID killed my business, we could start from scratch with more information, insight, and experience, as well as a better sense of what we did and did not want. It's not a situation we would choose, but it remains an opportunity whether invited or not. Destruction and opportunity travel together.

With my family dynamic changed, we had a blank slate from which to ask, *"What is it that we want to build here in this perceived void?"*

In May, less than two months after Dagny died, a friend messaged me and suggested I listen to a sermon from Pastor Steven Furtick called "Focus on the Fruit."

Listening as I walked along the canal, I rolled my eyes when he said, *"This might not be the prettiest time of my life, but it will be the most productive."*

I had no interest in productivity. Getting things done was the last thing on my mind. Is this what my friend wanted me to think about? Clearly, she'd never lost a child. I was spending hours a day sitting on the bathroom floor, staring blankly at the closet door. I was going into my office to scream and wail in private so I didn't scare or upset Chris.

Productive? Not a chance.

Fortunately, I kept listening long enough for a voice inside me to suggest, *"You're misunderstanding the word productive."*

For the longest time, I've thought of "productive" as getting lots of things done. A day is productive if, in addition to getting twenty things done at work, I've done three loads of laundry, cooked dinner, worked out, cleaned the kitchen, and organized the pantry.

In that dark, doubtful moment walking along the canal, I thought, *What if that's not it at all?* What if productivity doesn't have much to do with crossing things off the to-do list?

Before studying nutrition, I was a Latin and Greek major, so naturally, I love to think about the meaning of words and their origins.

I looked more closely at the word *productive* and immediately saw the root: produce.

What if productivity isn't about producing *any* result (laundry, phone calls, organization) but **producing something of value?**

More often than not, producing something of value is the exact *opposite* of getting lots of things done.

On the days where I've gotten lots of random things done, I've *rarely* produced something of value. All those little things I had been considering productive are generally insignificant and inconsequential. In fact, those random tasks tend to compete with and steal time and energy from my ability to produce something of value.

"This might not be the prettiest time of my life, but it will be the most productive."

With my reframe on the word productive, this idea started to take new shape. This time in my life might not be the prettiest, *but it might produce the most value.*

Maybe that's true. I don't have to invite these circumstances or want them, but this can be true even if I abhor the circumstances.

I turned this idea into a question that I've since come back to again and again:

What value can I produce for myself today?

What value can I produce for my health today?

What value can I produce for my family today?

What value can I produce for my marriage today?

What value can I produce for my team today?

What value can I produce for my faith today?

What value can I produce for my clients and listeners today?

What value can I produce from this pain?

What value can I produce from this loss?

What value can I produce from this experience?

What value can I produce from this loneliness?

Sometimes my answers are small and simple. I can make incredible food choices today. I can produce value for my health today by scheduling a doctor's appointment, taking a nap, massaging my scar, or taking my supplements. Sometimes they feel just a little bigger. I can ask Chris if he'd like to go for a walk or out on a date. I can record a podcast or reach out to a friend for support.

I've seen that, with almost every experience of pain or loss, we can uncover a seed of desire. The loss of a relationship can unearth a seed of desire for how you want your relationship to be. The loss of a job or a friendship might uncover a seed of longing for something familiar or something you've never had before but now value. These are productive realizations. *They're often how opportunity peeks through in the space you've experienced destruction.*

One morning, I journaled about the seed of desire for a large family that God planted within me as Dagny left us for Heaven. I thought about my responsibility to *do* something with it...my *opportunity* to do something with it. I have an opportunity to take action on it, continuously, and return to it again and again no matter how many times it seems to leave me.

Where have seeds of desire been planted in you? In that space of loss or destruction, what longing or wishing have you unearthed? Often, there's a seed of desire planted in the things we wish hadn't happened or the feelings we wish we hadn't felt.

Maybe you can recognize a seed of desire when you've felt jealous of another person's marriage, body, finances, or business. What is the seed of desire present in that moment you got angry at yourself for giving up or giving in?

Loss, real or perceived, often uncovers seeds of desire.

What will you do with them?

How will you nurture them?

I noticed, in the months following Dagny's death, how hard it became to communicate with Chris. We were grieving differently. Chris could compartmentalize things; I couldn't. I needed to talk about Dagny, her life and her death. Chris wanted to avoid those painful memories. Putting words to them was helpful for me and hurtful for him. The struggle uncovered the seed of desire—I wanted to connect, verbally, through this experience.

Painfully aware of our struggles to communicate verbally, I decided to buy a small notebook and write to Chris. I wrote a simple note, acknowledging this challenging season and our differing communication styles, expressing appreciation for the room we had given each other to grieve in our own ways. I asked him to write back to me.

I left it on his bedside table before I went to bed. The next morning, the small yellow notebook was on my bedside table. Inside was a second note, this one from Chris, with words of affection, encouragement, and hope.

For a few months, we wrote to each other regularly, passing the notebook back and forth every few days, helping us communicate in a time where verbal communication felt intensely strained.

Friend, this might not be the prettiest time of your life. Maybe you've been laid off, or your marriage has ended or is in jeopardy. Maybe you're struggling with infertility, or you're worried about a loved one. You could be in a fog of depression or feel alone or stuck.

I want you to know that though this is not the prettiest time of your life, it can be the time that produces the most value, and that often begins by recognizing the seeds of desire present in your pain.

The potential available in these times isn't passive. It requires your participation.

In Practice:

When you feel like something has been broken, damaged, removed, destroyed, or even simply changed in a way that you wish it wouldn't have changed, ask yourself: what do I want for this area of my life?

What is this loss or hardship showing you about the wants and needs you have?

What do you want to create here?

If you had a magic wand, what would you create in this void?

What's your role in that dream or vision?

Is there a small piece of it that you can implement today?

How can you produce value for your health today?

How can you produce value in a relationship today?

Begin to ask yourself to identify and act upon small ways you can add value.

THE POWER OF INVENTING

I'm on a bunch of different email lists but I have to say, I rarely open any of them. I probably delete 98 percent of the mass emails I get. For some reason, I opened an email from Tim Ferriss in early April 2020, less than a month after Dagny died. He shared a quote that encouraged me and challenged me.

*"After tragedies, one has to **invent a new world**, knit it or embroider, make it up. It's not gonna be given to you because you deserve it; it doesn't work that way. You have to **imagine something that doesn't exist** and dig a cave into the future and **demand space**. It's a territorial hope affair. At the time, that digging is utopian, but in the future, **it will become your reality**." (Emphasis mine)*

—BJÖRK

Yes, I have to invent a new world. The world with Dagny

in it doesn't exist anymore, at least not the way I thought it would.

We can read this quote as a mandate and a generous reminder of hope and possibility. I interpret it as an opportunity and as a responsibility.

I spent a lifetime imagining life with my first child.

I spent ten months imagining my life with Dagny.

I spent two weeks staring at her face and thinking of the life we would build together.

Now I'm building a foundation in her name and living life without her.

Invent a new world...it's an opportunity we **all** have all the time, irrespective of personal tragedy. It applies to you whether you've lost a loved one, lost a job, or are simply tired of being broke, lonely, or unhealthy.

In high school, I hated myself and my life. I didn't have many close friends; I was definitely the outsider in social circles. I was the fat kid. Every year, I planned to lose weight over the summer and go back to school transformed, but it never happened. Every summer, I gained more weight and dreaded going back to school. One summer, my mom and my aunt sat on the edge of my bed as I cried, and I remember my aunt telling me, *"You can always reinvent yourself. You can choose to be anyone you want to be."*

I found that so encouraging at the time. I could lose weight any time; the opportunity never expires. I could improve at sports, become an exceptional student, be a social butterfly, and build meaningful relationships.

Here I am again, decades later, needing to reinvent.

Before this great loss, I loved to complete the sentence, *"If everything is possible, I _____."*

This Björk quote feels a little like that, but more challenging.

What is the new world I want to invent?

"You have to imagine something that doesn't exist and dig a cave into the future and demand space."

Sometimes we have to (get to) do that in our personal lives.

Sometimes we have to (get to) do that in our families.

Sometimes we have to (get to) do that in our professional lives.

Sometimes we have to (get to) do that with our finances.

Imagine something that doesn't exist and dig a cave into the future and demand space.

Have a house full of children.

Have less stress.

Spend more time outside.

Laugh more.

Spend more time with family.

Travel more.

Transform my physical fitness.

We get to do this.

We can invent a new evening.

We can invent a new conversation.

We can invent a new opportunity.

A new relationship.

A new personality.

A new career.

Anything.

It's not going to come to us because we deserve it. We're going to have to dig a cave into the future and demand space.

It's work. It's worthwhile.

In this dark season where it feels easy to hyper-focus on what I lack, I remind myself that **I want to be the kind of person who lives with great expectations. I want to be the kind of person who has a mindset of abundance, even in seasons of loss or lack—the kind of person who sees possibility, especially in seasons when doors have been closed.**

Being positive has little merit when you're feeling optimistic. Being open to possibility isn't very impactful when your life feels fruitful. Seeking a perspective of abundance doesn't have much meaning when everything is going your way. These have the most power when you're in the trenches.

I can, and will, mourn Dagny while holding great expectations for my family's and my future. I can, and will, process pain, lack, and loss while seeking possibility and believing wholeheartedly in abundance.

It's not an easy choice, but it *is* a choice.

Some people stop at "not knowing." They stop at not knowing *what* they want to invent or how to get started. They stop at not knowing how to live in great expectation or not knowing how to seek possibility.

Not knowing was my initial instinct when I thought about this quote. I want my old life with Dagny. I don't want something new. I want something I can't have, so I guess I'm stuck. **But I wasn't stuck. I just stopped pursuing ideas.** I wasn't initially willing to do the work because I thought it meant letting go of the pain.

You aren't stuck either.

As I thought about it, my mind went to the old television set we had at our family beach cottage when I was a kid. We didn't have cable—the television signal was entirely dependent on the position of the two rabbit-ear antennae. They constantly had to be adjusted. Sometimes we'd even wrap aluminum foil around one or both ears to enhance the signal.

If we wanted to watch a show, we'd tinker endlessly until the signal came through. When it went out intermittently, we'd get back up and tinker again until the signal was strong again.

It made me wonder, *Am I willing to spend more effort on adjusting the TV antennae than my perspective to create a brighter future?*

I was so quick to stop at *"I don't know"* or *"This won't work"* when it came to improving my life, but I was more engaged in problem-solving and troubleshooting to get *Wheel of Fortune* to come through.

I don't want to be that person. I *can't* be that person if I want to live a great life (and I do want to live a great life).

Your first thought might feel like a dead end. It sure did for me. But it's no more of a dead end than the initial static you see on your old TV set.

We just have to keep adjusting.

Adjust your idea of options.

Adjust your sense of what is possible.

Rethink what your ideal is.

Wrestle with hard questions.

In Practice:

What do you want?

What else?

What do you want to create for yourself, your wealth, mindset, family, relationships, or career that doesn't yet exist?

In what way might you want to reinvent yourself?

What does it look like to *demand space* for these new things?

What would it look like if you lived with great expectations? Is there a way you can apply that today?

What viewpoints, perspectives, or practices do you need to adjust to bring these new thoughts into reality?

UNDERTHINKING

My husband, Chris, suffers from recurring tendonitis in his elbow. He enjoys CrossFit and has a very competitive mindset about lifting weights. He wants to "win" every workout, even if it hurts. With increasing frequency, the nagging pain in his elbow keeps him from a good workout.

We've learned his tendonitis doesn't flare up just because he lifts weights. In fact, the weight isn't the problem at all. It's *how he carries it*.

If he carries the weight poorly (bad form), he'll experience a lot of pain.

If he carries the weight well (good form), he can move with far less, if any, pain.

One night, as we were relaxing on the couch watching *Shark Tank* and Chris was rubbing his sore elbow, I reminded him about his form.

"It's not hurting simply because of what you're lifting. It's hurting because of how you're lifting it."

Having heard me say it a thousand times, Chris didn't respond (he's a smart man—he only responds to about half of the things I say). In the silence, I felt this subtle, internal prompting. What if this is also true for me? Does this apply metaphorically? How am *I* carrying this weight?

Maybe there's a way to carry the weight of this loss that inflicts less pain.

Maybe there's a way to carry the weight of this loss that inflicts *more* pain.

Honestly, I had never considered the possibility that there could be more than one way to carry grief. Then again, it took me about thirty years to acknowledge the many different ways to lose weight. I kept trying the same unsuccessful way for decades!

I thought back to years ago when my first husband and I divorced. I had a brand new business and, with the divorce, the safety net of my husbands salary and health insurance suddenly vanished. I was alone in an apartment with nothing but a bed and a chair. My family didn't live nearby, and we hadn't yet told our friends about our separation.

I wanted to revert to old "comforting" behaviors like binging on pizza and ice cream to numb out and escape some of the feelings. I distinctly remember telling myself, *"You can do that, but it won't make things better. It will make them worse."*

Yes, there is a way of carrying this grief that causes more pain.

At first, I didn't know the grief-carrying methods that reduced or alleviated pain, but we rarely need all the information to get started. **The first step is being open to the mere possibility of another way.**

To start, I could avoid the things that make it hurt more. Maybe that's all I had the power to change. Either way, I could start there.

At least a dozen times a day I remind myself: we either facilitate our healing, or we contribute to our demise. We either make time our friend, or we make time our enemy.

I have a few default settings in my life:

When stressed, distract/avoid/escape with food.

When hurting, withdraw.

Intellectually, I knew that overeating and pouring sugar and processed food into my body would not help. Intellectually, I knew that those things would make things worse. Biochemically, sugar is the ultimate bad mood food. Fueling my body with sugar and processed foods or overeating would lower my physical energy and emotional vibe.

As stress hormones surge, that imbalance influences all our other hormones. Overeating, sugar, and processed foods are stressors in and of themselves. While we might not feel the stress of overeating or excessive sugar consumption, they *are* physically stressful on the body.

Intellectually, you probably know these things too, but it's hard to think logically when emotions are on overdrive. Hard, yes. Impossible, no.

I reminded myself of these truths constantly. I would have an internal dialogue that went like this: *"This grief is bad. This pain is awful. I refuse to do anything to make it worse. With every choice—what I eat, watch on TV, or listen to; whether I get outside or not—I either contribute to healing or I don't. I either make time my enemy or I make time my friend. I either create a secondary problem or I don't. I either support my body or I don't."*

Ignoring my health or trashing my body would not only make me feel physically and emotionally worse, but it would also delay (at best) or impair (at worst) my physical healing.

In my decades-long struggle with food, I've learned I can never satisfy the wrong appetite. Some foods even increase your appetite! For years, when I had a subconscious appetite for peace, calm, or acceptance, I turned to food. It never satisfied. Some things leave you wanting more, feeling crappy, or both.

While I was writing this chapter, I got a text message from one of my clients. The day before, she shared a goal with me: she would never again eat chocolate. Her text let me know that she had received some bad news and hadn't followed through on her commitment to avoid chocolate.

I asked her what the news had to do with chocolate, or what story she told herself to make the news about chocolate. She quickly responded that she was stressed about the news and turned to the chocolate as a stress-reliever.

This is what I like to call *underthinking*.

Initially, it seems logical, but much of the truth is missing.

We can all convince ourselves that food will eliminate stress, spending money will bring joy, or binging on Netflix will help us relax. However, **convincing ourselves of some-**

thing doesn't make it true. There's often far more to the truth, but we just aren't demanding it from ourselves.

When we go along with an under-thought argument, we talk ourselves into false fulfillments and things that might meet a short-term need for distraction, but actually keep us from a long-term solution.

False fulfillments are little more than distractions.

In my relationship with my husband, I have developed a pattern of always having to prove a point. Often, I feel pretty certain my point is right and his is wrong, but taking the step to verbalize it is never fulfilling. However, I don't necessarily feel fulfilled when I avoid verbalizing my point or trying to be right. In fact, sometimes at first glance, it feels wrong to bite my tongue. It can feel like I missed an opportunity to show him the flaw in his logic. In the moment, I generally feel like he *needs* to see that flaw.

To make good decisions, we have to play it all the way out, staying mindful of the trap of underthinking.

Sure, it can give me a feeling of satisfaction to make a point or illuminate a flaw in Chris's argument or behavior, but then what?

What an awful relationship it creates to want to win more

than I want to connect and grow. My respect is more powerful than my point. Prioritizing connection over criticism helps us create the type of relationship we want to have. My willingness to not always feel right or try to win is more powerful than my point. This relationship is a partnership, not a battle. If I see it as winner/loser in a conversation, the relationship always loses.

There's so much more to the story than the initial underthought option.

We are either participating in the problem or the solution.

We have to play it out. We have to see it through to the theoretical end and consider the full scale of implications, not just our immediate thoughts or desires.

Practice ruthless objectivity.

Feelings aside, what's the best choice for my body?

I don't have to care. I don't have to want to or feel motivated. I practice ruthless objectivity.

You don't have to care.

You don't have to want to.

You don't have to be motivated.

You can practice ruthless objectivity.

Feelings aside, the best choice for my body might be to go for a walk.

Feelings aside, the best choice for my body might be green veggies and clean protein.

Though I don't want to make it, this choice fortifies my mind and body, thus supporting my healing. I regularly remind myself that the last thing I'm willing to do is make a bad situation worse.

Let me remind everyone (myself included) that this isn't black or white. I don't have to choose between watching *Investigation Discovery* or going for a five-mile walk. It's not *either* I eat pizza, sour watermelons, and Cheetos, *or* I have salmon and broccoli—open up to my friend *or* avoid her calls altogether.

In *Chasing Cupcakes*, I shared that one of my favorite mantras and personal reminders is that **binary is the opposite of creativity**.

"Binary" means having two parts: this or that, black or white, all or nothing. Binary choices reflect the opposite of creativity.

There are dozens, maybe even hundreds, of options that exist between all and nothing. *Underthinking is considering only the two most extreme or familiar options.*

It's not *either "I don't care" or "I'm motivated and engaged."* There's a massive gray area between those extremes, and it's a practice to consider the middle and opt into it.

Binary thinking is lazy thinking. It's turned-off, zero-effort thinking. It's underthinking.

Though our brains love to simplify with "this or that," life just doesn't work that way.

We have to embrace the reality that "both" almost always exists.

We have to embrace the reality that there's a massive scope of in-between options, too!

The goal isn't to find the *right* perspective. The goal is to invite *more* perspectives.

Overthinking

"Overthinking takes you to a place that doesn't exist."

—MAZEL J

We now know that underthinking comes from binary thinking, which can hold us back from growth and healing, but we also have to look at the way overthinking impacts our development.

Imagine putting your children or grandchildren to bed every night with a horror story of every worst-case scenario you can imagine.

"There once was a girl who totally dropped the ball. She screwed up over and over again. She lost her job, couldn't pay her bills, binged on junk food, and died alone."

It's a ridiculous thing to consider because you'd never tell your child a story like that, yet so many of us tell those kinds of stories to ourselves!

I'm probably going to lose my job.

What if I have cancer?

I'll probably just put all the weight back on, even if I do lose it.

What if I can't do it?

What if he cheats on me?

As we think those thoughts, we create a world that is pure illusion, manufactured by our undisciplined imagination. We let that undisciplined imagination create problems in our lives that look and feel real, but aren't.

One of the thoughts I manufactured in the early days of my grief was, *"What if Dagny isn't dead? What if they took her somewhere to recover and some other family is raising her now?"*

I am in control of whether or not I create and go down that rabbit hole. It's not happening to me; I either create it or I don't.

You are the thinker, not your thoughts. Unchecked and undisciplined, you can create a whole new type and brand of problem out of your own imagination.

As the powerful quote says, **overthinking takes you to a place that doesn't exist.**

When I was pregnant with Dagny, I remember going through all sorts of scary *"what ifs"* with my husband, Chris.

What if we don't get to the hospital in time when I go into labor?

What if she gets sick?

What if I experience postpartum depression?

He stopped me and very seriously asked, *"What if the house is on fire? How will you get out?"*

"The door in the kitchen," I replied.

"You can't," he said. *"It's blocked."* He said that of every other option I gave him until I shrugged in surrender and said, *"I guess I'd just die in here."*

He calmly replied, *"That is the first lesson I learned in basic training. Don't kill yourself with what-ifs."*

We are the thinkers. We are not the thoughts.

Overthinking takes you to a place that doesn't even exist.

Have you ever changed your plans after hearing the weather forecast?

You were going to go for a jog, but it's calling for rain, so you skip the run.

You didn't skip the run because it *is* raining but because it *might*.

You planned to work in the yard, but storms are in the forecast, so you put it off.

You didn't change your plans because it's storming but because it *might*.

What else have you not done because of "might"?

Might fail.

Might be hard.

Might not feel like it.

Might look stupid.

Might not work.

Might not last.

Is an imaginary scenario keeping you from an actual opportunity?

Too many of us are living behind imaginary walls we created by over- and underthinking. Actual barriers don't prevent us from taking action; imaginary barriers do.

Fear of judgment

Fear of criticism

Fear of failure

Fear of rejection

Doubt

Uncertainty

Past patterns

Friend, these aren't real walls. They only exist because you've manufactured them in your imagination! You've convinced yourself that something blocks your path, when there's nothing about it that could stop you other than your belief that it can.

In Practice:

Where are you prone to underthinking? Where are you going with your first thought or impulse? Why aren't you inviting the rest of the story to weigh in?

What else is true?

What have you left out?

What are you most likely to overthink about? Are there certain topics, situations, or areas of your life?

What "what ifs" are you willing to practice letting go of?

Where have you manufactured imaginary walls based on fear and doubt? Are these actual barriers or false walls? What else is true?

You might be wondering how you can stop these thoughts from arising in your mind. In my opinion, that's not the goal. Spontaneous thoughts will arise. You can't avoid them. It's about how you respond to them when they arise.

When the thoughts arise, how can you redirect to facts and away from worries?

LIVING IN THE LIMITATION

After Dagny died, I wanted to make some big, scary changes in my business. Unfortunately, I chose to focus on the dozens of reasons that these changes might not work, so I didn't make them. One day, it dawned on me that I hadn't given *nearly* as much time, energy, thought, effort, or attention to how or why they might work as I had given to how and why they wouldn't work. Right out of the gate I had focused on the risks and reasons it might fail, but I hadn't given equal (or greater) consideration to the potential upsides or ways to make it happen.

It's not the first time I had noticed this error in my thinking. A few years ago, I joined an elite business mastermind that felt far out of my league (and comfort zone). I left the first weekend workshop surprised by the number of people in the mastermind who were part of a network marketing business. For the vast majority of them, network marketing wasn't their primary business, but it was a strong source of additional income. To be honest, I thought they were crazy. I wondered, *"Why are they doing that crap when they're already successful in their other businesses? Don't they know better?"*

Frankly, I looked down on network marketing. I saw it as an inferior business model and couldn't wrap my mind around why it was so prevalent in this group of successful business owners. One of the women in the group even suggested that I consider it as an additional source of income, and I was steadfast in my belief that it was *not* for me.

After a few weeks of fixating on my low-level judgment and certainty that it wasn't for me, I realized that I had been giving disproportionate time, energy, thought, and attention to why it was a bad idea. What would it look like if I gave equal or greater attention to what might make it a great idea? I didn't have to decide to add it to my portfolio as an income stream, but the only way to become a better thinker is to **think beyond my biases**.

With that example in mind, I set out to think beyond my fear-driven biases around these big business changes I wanted to make. I set out to consider what it might take to make them work. I started sharing my idea with friends and colleagues and asking for their input. To my surprise, almost all of them encouraged me to go for it. Many of them pointed out the advantages and upsides I hadn't considered because I was focused on doubt and fear of failure.

In a matter of a week, I shifted from having counted the idea out to being certain that it was the exact path I needed to take and feeling excited about all the doors it might open.

This shift happened only because I was willing to think differently. It only happened because I realized that I was favoring doubt and fear to the exclusion of possibility, ingenuity, and creativity.

I know I'm not alone in the tendency to count out an idea or path because you settle on all the reasons it won't work without giving equal or greater consideration to why it might work. I know I'm not alone because I hear about it from my listeners and clients every week.

I can't build a business because I don't have a big enough network. I can't do it because I wouldn't even know where to start. I can't do it because I don't have enough time, I don't have enough money, I'm too young, too old, too inexperienced. I can't do it because it's already been done before.

I can't lose weight because I'm inconsistent and I give up easily. I can't lose weight because I've already tried everything and it hasn't worked. I can't lose weight because my hormones are out of whack, my life is too crazy, or I give in when confronted with temptation.

I can't travel, have a cleaning lady, or invest in real estate because I don't make enough money or my bills are too high.

I'm not here to tell you those aren't real circumstances. More often than not, our perceived limitations *do* stem from past patterns and historical fact.

It might be very true that your hormones are out of whack. You have a small network or you don't know how to build a business.

And: those aren't fixed points. They aren't static. You can change them. You can overcome them. You can balance your hormones. You can build your network and/or you can make your idea work with a small network. You can learn how to build a business. You can create consistency. *It is all possible*, even if you choose not to do it. After Dagny's death, I had all the reasons in the world to not make a massive shift in my business. Eliminating 95 percent of my revenue during a global pandemic might be called foolish. My new ideas might not even work! And yet, it was entirely possible that it would work and it would make space for something even better!

Stop living in the limitation. Refuse to lock into your first idea, especially when it's rooted in assumption, fear, past patterns, or insecurity.

No matter how many times you've struggled to lose weight

or you've broken promises to yourself: you can change that pattern. You are not, in any way, limited by the way things have been.

We are most susceptible to locking into limitation when life feels hard. It doesn't matter if you're simply stressed about work, overtired, or walking through job loss, divorce, or grief. This is when we need to be most on guard against this pattern.

Let me tell you a story about a conversation I recently observed in the Primal Potential Facebook group. Upon starting to read my first book, *Chasing Cupcakes*, a woman shared the following in the free group:

"I've started Chasing Cupcakes *and there is a statement in the beginning part of the book that says, 'information isn't transformation.' Guilty. As. Charged. I **love** acquiring new information...and then not applying it. Elizabeth's got my number!!! Anyone else?"*

The comments started pouring in:

Me!

150 percent me!

Totally me!

I'm guilty as well.

Yep, that would be me. I'm not a doer.

I was jumping out of my skin as I read the comments.

You cannot and will not step into a new pattern of behavior if you're still claiming the old one! You cannot and will not step into a new version of yourself if you're still *agreeing* with and identifying with the old one!

Maybe you have failed to implement before, but my friend, that has *nothing* to do with today! You are free to be a master implementor or action taker today, *but you won't* if you're identifying with the way you operated yesterday!

Each person saying *"Yes, that's me"* regarding a past pattern is choosing to invest in predictability instead of possibility.

Where do you go, in your thoughts, when you recognize a problem or feel frustration? Do you go to the past, or do you go to the present? Do you go to the problem, or do you go to the solution? Do you think in terms of predictability or possibility?

This is what I'm talking about when I refer to the critical importance of becoming a better thinker.

If you claim the past as your present pattern, you will keep it as your present pattern.

You are not in any way limited by the way things have been *unless* you still connect to it with your thoughts, identity, and beliefs!

You can make more money. It's never been more accessible. It doesn't matter how old you are, how many jobs you have, or how much education you have. Every single one of us can make more money. You are *not* limited by how much you make, even though you convince yourself that you are.

You can lose weight, no matter how many times you've failed.

You can build that business.

You can take the time off.

You can create a strong network.

There is a way. You might not know what it is and you might not believe in your ability to do it, but even those aren't real limitations. You might choose to stop there, but you don't *have* to stop there.

Refuse to continue living in the limitation.

Whatever it is, life is short. Find a way and make it happen!

So many of us are being **loyal to a lie** especially when life feels hard. We accept the limitation without equal or greater consideration given to what else might be true. In doing so, we limit our thinking and we limit our range of possible outcomes. We limit our possible outcomes to our past, our fears, doubts, and insecurities.

I was being loyal to the lie that I couldn't take time off, I couldn't take time to focus on just the podcast and the book. I focused on every reason that supported why I couldn't do those things. I didn't focus on any of the reasons I could do those things.

I see this when I hear people talking about how they can't afford a particular dream or they don't have time or they can't lose weight or get fit.

They are being loyal to a lie. It is possible.

Stop accepting the status quo. **Stop limiting your life to the bounds of your creativity.**

Be creative. Decide to be a creative, energetic problem solver.

Stop letting "no" win. Stop letting fear win. Stop letting your past, your doubts, or your uncertainty be a barrier. It's a choice.

Be creative in how you make money.

In your work.

In your relationships.

Be creative in how you think.

Don't remain in an echo chamber, thinking about things the way you always have.

Thinking about food the way you always have.

Thinking about money the way you always have.

Thinking about relationships the way you always have.

Thinking about politics the way you always have.

Choose to view things from possibility instead of pattern and predictability. **The "how" can always be figured out!**

In Practice:

What do you feel is off-limits, unlikely, impossible, or out of bounds?

What do you think you can't do?

Where have you argued for what is in your way or holding you back?

Talk to a minimum of five people who have done what you want to do. Where did they start? What did they learn? What mistakes did they make? What advice do they have? How might they do it differently if they were starting over?

What evidence exists in support of your ability to do it?

What evidence needs to exist?

Can you create the evidence?

What mindset or perspective would you need to have to believe you can do it?

Where do you need to give more time, energy, thought, attention, or effort to what is possible?

RESPONDING INTELLIGENTLY

About three weeks after Dagny died, my sister texted me a link to an article she thought might help me. It was a Dear Sugar column featuring a letter from an angry father who had lost his son.

Though it didn't make me feel any better about Dagny's death, it did give me an idea of how to work through some of my hardest thoughts.

A man, deeply grieving his son, had written to Sugar to share many of his thoughts around his loss. He wrote about not being able to stand the pain, not wanting to live without his son, and being tormented by thoughts of the man who had killed him by driving drunk.

Sugar replied in kind with a list of *other* thoughts. She wrote about the obliterated place that exists in you after such a loss. She wrote about learning to live with the pain and the loss and working to make something beautiful in the obliterated place.

For me, it felt too soon to walk the path of making something beautiful, though maybe these very words I'm typing are the creation of a beautiful thing.

I could, however, relate to living in the obliterated place. I could relate to the idea of being a mom but not a mom.

The format of the article offered me, and you, a tool to use: a thought and a response to the thought.

This came up the other night on a live webinar I hosted. During the Q&A, a woman unmuted herself and said, *"How can I stop feeling so resentful of the work I feel like I have to do?"* When I asked her to clarify, she explained that she wants to lose weight and work out more consistently, but she feels like she's constantly having to do the work to think differently about those decisions and she resents the constant effort.

I'll tell you what I told her. That is one perspective and it's valid. However, it's not the only perspective. You can convince yourself that it's a drag, that you don't want to do it and shouldn't have to. There's also more to the story, whether you decide to tell it or not.

Your initial resistance to the effort is your first thought, but you don't need to let it be your last. This Dear Sugar article reminded me of that valuable lesson and practice.

I don't want to be owned or led by my first thought. I want to allow space to *respond* to the thought. I want to give enough time for a more balanced thought to arrive. I want to be in a habit of inviting my own second opinions.

In grief, my first thoughts are painful. They're often sad, angry, and desperate. Sometimes, my second and third thoughts are, too, but often they have more space, more breathing room, more patience, and more light. My second thoughts often reflect more possibility.

In the first few weeks after Dagny died, I wasn't inviting any space for the response to a thought. I rushed from one jagged thought to another, like tumbling through white-water rapids and getting tossed between angry water and rocks.

After reading the article, I wrote down some of my most prevalent thoughts and took the time to create a response to the thought and invite other thoughts instead of pressing forward with my initial opinion. My goal was simply to leave space for my own second opinion.

First thought: I can't live without her.

Second thought: Do you have one more second in you? And wait...before you say you don't know if you do, before you say you can't handle another second, just wait one second.

In that waiting, that's your surviving.

You don't have to *think* you can do it, just allow the painful moments to happen.

That's your passage through this unbearable space.

You don't have to have words for it.

You don't have to agree with it.

Just wait a second. Take a breath.

Keep taking one hard, tentative breath at a time.

And stay there, like that, for as long as you need to.

The way things feel in this moment isn't the way they will feel for the eternity of moments. No season lasts forever.

First thought: I miss her so badly it hurts. I've never imagined pain like this. I've never screamed for someone, until now. This dark pain, it sits there waiting for me to wake up in the morning. It never leaves. It's a dark shadow no one else can see or feel.

Second thought: I know. The only thing bigger, stronger, and more powerful than that all-consuming grief is your never-ending love for her. And that's a beautiful testament to the unbreakable bond between you and your daughter. Remember: the intensity of grief is a reminder of how much love you have for Dagny. You know what else is beautiful? All she ever felt in her life was your epic love. She never knew heartbreak. She never knew loneliness. Remember the courage of the seed.

First thought: I will never stop blaming myself. I must have missed something. There was a sign we didn't see. What could we have done differently? If we had done it, Dagny would still be here.

Second thought: What you're doing here is one of the hardest parts of grief. Allow yourself to question. Allow yourself to be angry. Take steps to get answers. Talk about it. You're still trying to protect her, even after she's gone. It's a beautiful and agonizing way you love Dagny. I'm so sorry it won't bring her back. Ignore everyone who says, *"You can't do that to yourself."* You can. It's part of your process, so allow for these thoughts.

First thought: I'm angry about the way some people have and haven't responded. I feel like I see everyone in my life differently now. I feel like there's so much more than just one loss. We lost Dagny and that's the worst kind of pain I never imagined, but there's this other unspoken loss. The loss you feel when someone close to you doesn't even call upon hearing that you lost your child. The loss you feel when that close friend never texts to say, *"What do you need? How can I help?"* I feel like my world is the tiniest fraction of the size it once was.

Second thought: I can't make that right for you. But you could crystallize and reinforce the way you want to love and support people who are struggling as you go forward. Anger is part of grief. Give the hurt relationships some time. You don't have to make decisions or declarations right now. Right now, you have to let the grief feel and be however it shows up. In time, it might look different. And it might not. But for now, these feelings are part of the journey. Let it be what it is and be open to knowing that it will likely shift and change with time.

First thought: I don't want to laugh. I don't want to talk about anything other than Dagny. It feels like a betrayal. Like someone might think I'm not in agony. It makes me crazy when people who know I've lost my girl, say *"Have a great day"* or *"I hope you're doing well."* My days are so far from great. I'm barely alive. I'm not doing well. I can't imagine being worse. I want to reply, *"Seriously? Clearly, you've never watched your child die."*

Second thought: You know, they probably *haven't* ever watched their child die. Thank God. And a few weeks ago, you hadn't either. **Don't expect your level of understanding from them.**

This Dear Sugar article reminded me of the work I do with my clients every day. Don't rely on your first thought. Create a habit of asking, *"What else is true? Is there a better version of this story? Is there a thought that feels better?"* Leave room for a second thought, a more rational thought, or a less impulsive thought.

That doesn't mean the first thought is wrong; it probably isn't wrong at all. But it's not the only thought. It's not the only perspective.

Have you ever heard the quote *"A lie makes its way halfway around the world before the truth gets its pants on"*?

I think about that a lot.

I can be full-on into acting on my first thought before I ever give consideration to the fact that there might be another idea or another perspective or a more balanced or fully honest perspective.

Give room and space for your first thoughts, but don't let them be your *only* thoughts. Leave space and time for a response to those thoughts.

I've shared this story a million times on the podcast, but I think of it and use it so often I'll share it again here.

When Chris and I first moved into our farmhouse, built in 1707 and in major need of updating, I was standing outside with one of Chris's very artistic uncles, sharing a bunch of my ideas.

He said to me, *"That's a really good idea. But never go with your first idea."*

That proved to be so true in design and renovation. We had a lot of good ideas and a lot of bad ideas. Giving those ideas time, giving them consideration, and asking ourselves (and experts) what other options we might have always brought us to a better idea.

One of our first ideas on how to renovate the first floor included gutting and totally remodeling the downstairs bathroom. It was necessary, it was a good idea, and the new layout would have been such an improvement. But our second idea, to relocate the bathroom to the other side of the house so we had a more open living area, was an even better idea.

This is a practice you can apply to all your thoughts. Often, my first thought when seeing Chris's dirty socks on the floor is, *"Are you kidding me? Again?"* As small as this scenario is in the scheme of life, it's how I practice for the bigger things. I choose to invite other thoughts. Having Chris here isn't a guarantee—I've seen that prove itself true in life. Maybe I can appreciate these little signs of life and presence. And, in the scheme of things, is it really worth *any* degree of annoyance, no matter how minor? **Is that the threshold I have for annoyance? If socks on the floor is all it takes to ruffle my feathers, I'm in trouble.**

Give your first thoughts a little time, space, and consideration.

While I was writing this chapter, I had a particularly challenging day. I had been up most of the night after a recurring traumatic nightmare. Then, I spilled my hot mug of tea all over myself and the floor. I went the wrong way on the highway and got stuck in traffic I never should have been in and ended up late for an appointment. On top of that, we ran into a bunch of work issues, so my texts and emails were blowing up.

Later that afternoon, I logged into Facebook to review my client groups and saw a quote posted by one of my longtime clients. It said:

What's the best that could happen?

That single perspective snapped me out of my myopic focus on everything that had gone wrong earlier in the day. It brought me back to the present and shifted my perspective in a powerful way.

Your first thought might be of worry. Your first thought might be of loss, stress, fear, or lack.

That's okay. It's not bad or wrong. *You're* not bad or wrong. I'm simply suggesting that you leave room to consider, what's the best that could happen?

Just a few hours after seeing that quote on a challenging day, a friend texted me. Knowing the tough season I'm in, she asked, *"Has anything in particular brought you hope today?"*

I shared how that one question had come at just the right time as it got me thinking about the very best that could happen. In response, she shared yet another powerful question:

Is there a better version of this story I could tell?

I'll be honest...if I heard that question when Dagny first died, I would have said *"No."* With conviction, I would have told you there's no better story. It's just tragic, painful, and life altering.

Now, a few months removed, I can tell you that yes, it's tragic, it's painful, it's life altering. It's also life *expanding*.

I don't regret carrying Dagny. I loved every second of being pregnant. I don't regret having her for fourteen days. Yes, I wanted it to be my entire lifetime, but fourteen days with her were a gift. Seeing Chris with her changed my life in a wonderful way. I will live life better and I will be a better mother because of our experience with Dagny.

It's not only tragic. Yes, it's tragic. It's also beautiful.

What else is true?

How else can you see this?

In Practice:

Respond to your own thoughts, small and large, significant and insignificant.

What else is true? What other perspectives can I invite?

What other ideas do I have about this?

If you have a thought about being angry, how might you respond to that thought?

How would you respond if you were calm and rational?

How would you respond if you were giving advice to someone else?

How would you respond if you were happy?

How would you respond if you were giving yourself all the time the world?

What's a calmer thought?

What's a more rational thought?

What's a kinder thought?

What's a more balanced thought?

What's a more mature thought?

THEY CAN'T GET IT

Aside from coping with the reality of losing Dagny, one of the hardest things for me to work through in this last year has been my pain surrounding the actions and inactions of people in my life. We don't live in a bubble. When we're going through a hard time, other people are part of the story, usually in ways we can't control.

The shutdown and fears that came with COVID-19 coincided with Dagny's death, resulting in unexpected isolation and lack of support. Having grown up in a family that modeled support in a very consistent way, I struggled with seeing how reality differed from my expectations. It felt like I had been served a harsh reality about how many people actually cared about us.

I know I'm not alone in the pain that comes from how we receive and perceive the actions and inactions of others.

I'd be lying if I told you I'm over this or that I have perfect tools for navigating these situations. However, there are a handful of tools I turn to when I find myself deep in the hurt of things that have been said, done, not said, or not done.

My first approach is to remind myself that **other people can't share my perspective because they don't share my experience.** My perspective comes from my experience and their perspective comes from their experience. I remember thinking, *"Never in a million years would I call someone who just lost a child and tell them how their grief or their way of grieving hurt my feelings. It would just never, ever happen."* However, that perspective of mine comes from someone who just lost a child. I can't take my perspective, which stems from my experience, and assume that someone who *doesn't* have that experience will share that perspective.

They can't. They won't.

The real issue is my expectation that their perspective will match mine. *It can't.*

I feel strongly that if someone I love lost a child, I'd drive through fire, I'd show up in a full hazmat suit if needed, but I'd be there. I'd stay six feet or twelve feet or one hundred feet away if that's what made me feel safe, but come hell or high water, they would see me. Again however, that perspective comes from someone who just lost a child and had staggeringly few people show up. I can't reasonably hold someone who *hasn't* had that experience to the expectation that comes from living it and breathing it and feeling the pain of it.

Their perspective is different. My perspective is different. Your perspective is different. As much as I would love for my family and friends to share my perspective, they can't.

That realization does not always take away the pain or the sting of our differing perspectives, at least not for me, but it is a helpful reminder and powerful practice.

Have you ever heard the parable of the blind men and the elephant? It tells the story of a group of blind men who heard that an elephant had been brought to their small village. Not knowing what an elephant was, they went into town to find out for themselves.

One of the men approached the elephant and grabbed its trunk. Exploring the trunk with his hands, he announced to the other blind men that an elephant was similar to a large, thick snake. Another of the blind men grabbed onto the elephant by its ear and argued with the first man. *"It's nothing like a snake! It's like a fan or a large, strong leaf!"* A third blind man placed his hands on the elephant's tusk and of course thought the others were crazy. An elephant is smooth and hard like a spear!

None of the men were wrong, but none of them were entirely correct either. They were drawing conclusions from their experiences, which is what we all do, often not realizing that just like there are other parts of an elephant, there are other parts of an experience that make it look quite different! These blind men made a mistake in assuming that their perspective was the *only* perspective.

This has been one of the most valuable tools I use when in conflict with others. I'm looking at my experience, which they didn't have. I'm considering my feelings, which they don't feel. They're looking at their experience, which I didn't have. They're considering their feelings, which I don't feel. I don't have to assume that my perspective is the only perspective or the only right perspective.

It's *always* this way. We get to choose that reminder. **We get to opt in to that truth.**

In some relationships, we can successfully share our views and our perspectives and make progress. But listen, as hard as it is, sometimes people will *only* see their own perspective. They don't want to hear that there is in fact a desk because they don't see a desk and they're committed to *their* viewpoint. Everything else doesn't exist because they can't see it.

Sometimes **you** are that person, but you can't see it, because you're certain that what you see is the only truth.

There are always different viewpoints, and it's rare that *any* of them are entirely wrong.

It might be an easier world if everyone realized their view isn't the only view or the right view, but it's never going to be that way with everyone at every point in time. We can only work on ourselves. Our view isn't their view. We can't expect our level of understanding from anyone else because they don't have our view.

Have you ever heard of a children's book called *Zoom*? Each page contains just one picture. The first picture is this red pointy thing; it looks like a random triangle.

When you turn the page, the picture has zoomed out. Now, and only now, you see that red pointy thing is a rooster's comb.

With each turn of the page, the image zooms out further. After just a couple pages, you don't even see the red triangle or the rooster, though both are still there.

I feel like this resembles life, except we don't always turn the page. We don't always zoom out or step back for the wider view, even though the wider view shows a very different picture.

Without stepping back, without zooming out, we are *sure*

we see a red triangle. We are certain there isn't a rooster, and if you suggest that there is in fact a rooster, you're crazy.

Without zooming out, we are sure we see offense. We are sure we see selfishness. We are sure we see something that would certainly look different if we zoomed out.

We can choose to seek the whole picture, and if we would only insist that we step back and zoom out, we might see something very, very different.

It's not that you're wrong in what you see, it's that there's much more to it!

Slow down. Step back. Zoom out.

Often, what's missing from our perspective is context. That context might require someone else's perspective, additional information, or the mere passage of time.

The other day, I sat in Dagny's nursery for the first time since she died. In fact, I hadn't been in there since before she was born. We had her downstairs with us the entire time she was home. It was so painful. I sat on the floor thinking, *"It shouldn't be this way."*

In the context of what *I* know and in the context of where I am in my life journey, this is the worst possible thing. This isn't what I'd choose. But I only have my context. I can only see things as they are right now.

I'm lacking the context of my future and what happens next. I'm lacking the context of the lifelong impact of The Dagny Foundation. I'm lacking God's context.

It's a dangerous thing to draw conclusions or make decisions without context.

If someone gives me attitude and I conclude that they're rude or they don't like me, I've overlooked their context. *The* context. My perspective isn't the same as objective or complete context. Maybe they're tired. Maybe they got bad news today. Maybe I hurt them in some way and they haven't shared that with me.

The worst decisions come when we take things out of context.

When Chris shuts down in a conversation and I think he's being immature or dismissive, tensions often rise. But I'm operating without complete context. It could be that he's not sure of how to communicate about this topic. It might not be a good time for him to get into it. He could be afraid, tired, or feeling attacked. Complete context is critical, and when we operate without it, we're taking a big risk.

When someone swerves off the road in front of me, before I get irritated, I need to remember that I don't have their context. They could be having a heart attack. Their car could be malfunctioning.

The tricky thing about context is that we can't always have it.

Fortunately, we can recognize when we don't.

I don't have God's context for my life.

I can't have the context of the other drivers on the road.

I don't have the context that only the passage of time can deliver.

When I acknowledge that, I'm less likely to judge others. I'm less likely to jump to conclusions. I'm less likely to get upset.

It's easy to judge situations and people when we don't have context. It's easy to operate exclusively from our own perspective, but it's destructive.

Are you assuming the best or the worst?

Are your assumptions fear based or faith based?

Are your thoughts hopeful or harmful?

Are they aligned with your past or your potential?

We can practice this in big situations and small.

Let's say you want ice cream tonight. What context do you put around that decision? You deserve it? It won't hurt? You'll feel better if you don't? Your body doesn't need more fuel right now?

When it comes to other people—strangers, partners, kids, friends—it's easy to judge when we lack their context.

Someone is standoffish. They didn't text you back. They didn't invite you. What context do you create? What assumptions do you make?

We will make the worst decisions of our lives when we jump to conclusions without context.

Practicing perspective and seeking complete context will not only upgrade your mindset, it will enhance your relationships. In every situation, what you see is based on your perspective, which comes from your experience and the context you create.

In Practice:

Where are you feeling angry or hurt by how someone else doesn't share your perspective?

Where do you expect people to understand your perspective?

In what situations are you holding resentment because people don't share your perspective?

Work on developing a narrative that, instead of convincing you of the validity of your anger, convinces you that you are the only one who can possibly understand your feelings and actions.

Practice giving people grace when they see things differently. Expect it.

Implement a practice of saying to others, *"Tell me how you see this"* without countering with your own perspective.

Imagine that every scenario in your life is like that children's book *Zoom,* because it is. You see what you see, and you know there is much more to the picture that you can't yet see.

CENTER OF THE STORY

About four weeks after Dagny died, a woman sent me a direct message via Instagram. I didn't know her, but after listening to the podcast and following me on social media, it seemed like she thought she knew me.

In her message, she shared about a loss she had in her life and how she went back to work too soon and regretted it.

At the end of her message she said, *"I urge you to step back from your work, Elizabeth. It will be there when you get back. You need to take time to grieve."*

I initially felt irritated when I read it. My first thoughts reflected my pain and disappointment that someone would (a) offer unsolicited advice about how I should handle my grief without having a personal relationship with me and (b) suggest that working in a very limited capacity meant I was not making time for my grief.

I handled my grief moment by moment in the way that felt right for me, and her projection felt out of bounds. I responded with what I felt reflected a balance of clear boundaries, addressing assumptions, and empathy. I acknowledged that her message surely came from a great place but that she simply didn't know enough about my work, my life, my grief to make a recommendation about what I *should* do.

My response didn't land well with her. She replied that she clearly didn't know me and had someone given *her* that advice when she lost someone in her life, she would have been gracious and grateful. She told me not to message her again and that she wouldn't listen to my podcast anymore.

For several hours, I felt hurt by her reaction to my reply. I played it over in my head a dozen times. How could she not see that she had made assumptions? How could she not see that sending unsolicited advice to a grieving stranger might not be a good idea?

At the time, the very last thing I needed was another thing to be upset about. I already carried a heavier burden than I could manage with the pain of my loss; I knew I needed to find a way to release this interaction and end my perseveration on it.

I reminded myself that I get to choose how I interpret her

message, and my chosen interpretation will determine how I feel. These are decisions.

What actually happened? What story, if any, do I create? How much emotion do I infuse into the interaction?

From there, I remind myself to remove me from the center of the story. To do that, it helps to simplify. In this case, a stranger offered advice reflecting her journey without insight into my reality and I don't agree with her advice. The end. I don't have to infuse it with any drama. Initially, I chose to be offended. It wasn't a wrong or unsubstantiated choice, but it also wasn't my *only* choice.

Recently, a client texted me during a tough moment for her. Separated from her husband and knowing divorce was imminent, she found out that her husband was seeing someone and wanted their child to meet this new person.

She shared with me that this must be the reason he's eager to file for divorce quickly. She fought the urge to turn to food as an escape from her emotion. We used our exchange as an opportunity to simplify. Here's exactly what I shared with her:

> *"I'd encourage you to not draw conclusions or make assumptions. Deal with facts. He wants your daughter to meet someone new to you. The rest is invented."*

She could put herself at the center of the story, but she can also put facts at the center of the story. She can put her daughter at the center of the story. She can put her ex at the center of the story.

We can practice identifying what is invented or assumed and setting that aside so we have a simpler view.

We have options, and it's incredibly valuable to practice not putting ourselves at the center of every story. It goes a long way towards minimizing conflict and unwanted emotions.

In Practice:

Ask yourself: with my current perspective, who do I have as the center of the story?

What would it look like to remove yourself from the center of the story?

How can you be more understanding of someone else's perspective?

Is there a way you can invite their perspective to round out your own?

Is this worth being offended about? Why? What are your other choices?

Who or what else could you put at the center of the story?

How can you simplify what is happening?

What does it look like through facts, without feelings?

What if you were to strip away all the context you added?

What have you invented?

CLEANING THE FOREST

A day or two after Dagny's funeral, Chris and I went up to my family's home in the mountains of Maine. Honestly, I wanted to hop on a flight far, far away but didn't have that option due to the pandemic. In a house without television or internet, with the entire country closed down, all we did was rest, think about Dagny, walk outside, and play the occasional card game.

One afternoon, I forced myself to go for a walk. A river coursed on my left, and a forest stood on my right. At one point, I looked to my right and saw chaos of fallen trees, broken branches, and dead leaves.

I said to Chris, *"That's what my life feels like right now. It feels as impossible as it would feel if someone pointed to the forest and said, 'Clean it up.'"*

It reminded me of this often-used story about a man who wanted to get into real estate and to have the money to do so, he had to sell his truck. Upside down in his loan, he didn't even know where to start. He needed to take so many steps to get out from under the truck, financially speaking.

He slowed down enough to think, *"Well, before I can do anything, I need to clean the truck."* So he cleaned it.

He realized, *"Before I can list it for sale, I'll need photos."* He grabbed his camera and took the pictures.

Small step by small step, he navigated all the things that needed to be done.

I remember moving into an apartment many years ago and feeling overwhelmed by unpacking my closet. It felt like I would never finish. I grabbed one small pile of clothes, maybe just ten or twelve items, and reframed the entire project. Instead of setting out to unpack the entire closet, I folded or hung this small pile. I did that a few more times before taking a break, and that approach turned the task from overwhelming to completely manageable.

It would be the same approach if I were tasked with cleaning the forest. Sure, I could stand there and convince myself that it's impossible, or I could fill one bag with leaves.

I'd probably need a chain saw. I've never used a chain saw.

But before I figure all that out, I'd have to get one. I am capable of buying or borrowing a chain saw.

So it is with life. So it is with grief.

We can look at it and convince ourselves that progress is impossible. Or we can identify the smallest next step and take it. Then, we do it again. Just start. Anywhere.

I think about this in terms of my relationship with Chris. Honestly, I don't know how to navigate losing a child, during quarantine, with a man who experiences emotion so much differently than I do. It feels like cleaning the forest.

But I can smile at him when I go inside. I can hug him and tell him I love him.

Get that next piece of information.

Try this new thing.

Eat that salad.

Put down the remote.

Pray. Write. Walk. Ask.

What is your next small step?

The other day, I got a text from a client of mine. She shared that she needs to make more time for herself. But, she continued, she has two grown kids, a husband, and grandchildren she routinely cares for, one of whom has special needs. She went on and on about all the details of the problem and what impeded the solution she sought. She shared the guilt she would feel if she couldn't be there for her grandchildren because of a poor diet and lack of exercise.

She wanted to clean the forest, but instead of focusing on *how* to clean the forest or where she could start, she told me about how many trees stood in the way and how many thousands of leaves lay on the ground.

She asked me for suggestions of affirmations to help her believe that she can care for herself, but honestly, I think that's like asking for belief you can clean the forest. That's not what you need. You don't have to believe you can do it, you just have to start. Belief can be built along the way.

Instead, I asked her what changes she wanted to make and see. She explained that two of the biggest shifts she wanted to make were related to consistently eating better and working out.

Guiding her focus, I asked, *"What can you do to create an improvement in one or both of those areas today?"*

She talked about indulging less. She can do that today, even if she's caring for everyone else. There's nothing about caring for everyone else that removes her ability to indulge less.

I return to this strategy every day. I use it when I'm writing the pages of this book, when the kitchen is a disaster, when I want to lose weight, grow my business, or navigate the trenches of grief.

What's the first step, and am I willing to take it right now? That's the only helpful place to focus.

In Practice:

What feels overwhelming? It doesn't matter if it's as trivial as cleaning the kitchen or if it's as significant as living through grief. Begin by identifying what feels like an impossible undertaking.

Next, identify some of the pieces. You don't have to break down every step in the process, but break it down into at least a handful of smaller pieces.

Look for major and minor moments of overwhelm. Practice isolating one part of the project and getting that done before moving on to another isolated part.

When you practice in the small things, you're more equipped to practice in the big things.

HARD TO BREATHE

On every walk since Dagny died, I cry. On one particular walk, I cried so hard that it became hard to breathe. My breaths were shallow, and even though I'm sure I *was* breathing, I wasn't getting in enough air.

Sarcastically I thought, *"Great, I'm going to faint out here at 6 a.m. and no one will ever find me. It's gonna be a good day."*

My struggle to breathe continued for about a minute before I realized that I was kind of holding my breath. Not fully, but I couldn't take more air in because I hadn't released the air from the last breath.

If you don't empty your lungs, you can't fill them. If you don't exhale fully, you can't inhale fully.

Intentionally and desperately, I pushed out all the air I could. Sure enough, my very next breath felt complete. I didn't have to struggle to inhale anymore; it happened automatically as soon as I forced myself to let go.

There are countless lessons and tools in this.

If you don't let go, you can't receive.

Sometimes, when something feels hard, it might not be that it *is* hard; it might be that we haven't let go of the last thing. You're carrying too much. You haven't created enough space.

Think about it this way: picking up a grocery bag isn't hard unless you are already holding twelve.

Inhaling isn't hard, unless you haven't exhaled.

The primary thing that this struggle to breathe taught me is that exhaling doesn't mean you don't value air. Exhaling doesn't mean you don't care or you're over it.

It doesn't mean you think you don't need air or that you don't want air or that you're okay with not having it at all.

You exhale so that you can inhale. You release so that you can receive.

You know you need more, and you acknowledge that the

only way to get more of what you need is to let go of what you just had.

Exhaling means you know there's more, *even when more is different.*

I have resisted and resented the notion of letting go of so much that has surrounded this loss. I haven't wanted to let go of the anger towards other people, of the traumatic moments that play on repeat in my mind, or of the constant focus on loss. I've repeatedly told myself letting go means saying goodbye to those memories or not caring about them anymore. I mistakenly thought that letting go was synonymous with eliminating.

Confronted with this example of breathing, I see how not true that is, and I'm grateful for it.

I'm not eliminating oxygen when I exhale. I'm not living without it. I'm making room for more. I had to ask myself, *"Wait. Am I saying that letting go of anger means making room for more anger?"* Maybe. But I don't think that's the true issue.

The issue is holding on so tightly. It prevents flow. It's restrictive and constricting. Holding on and refusing to release makes you feel like you can't move or can't breathe.

Sometimes we think that letting go means not caring or not

valuing that thing we need to let go of. It doesn't. Letting go is the way we open ourselves up to be refilled.

Sometimes, I use prayer for this. One of my family members said something to me after Dagny died that pops into my mind regularly and brings up feelings of anger and defensiveness. There is a softening perspective I could choose, but how I choose to release this particular one is prayer. Every time that memory resurfaces, I pray, *"God, please release that memory from my mind. Please take away my anger. I don't want to be mad. I don't want to have division in that relationship."*

There are so many ways to practice letting go, but it's that word, practice, that is the key. You can't simply desire to let go. You have to practice. You have to participate. You have to put forth effort. Choose a new perspective, turn to prayer, meditate, or visualize the response you want to have.

I believe that begins with looking at where you're holding on and *wanting* to release. Sometimes, we just want to be mad. Sometimes, we don't want to let go of that thing that makes our blood boil. Personally, I think that's fine. Practice with something you *are* willing to let go of. That's where the work begins. You get out of your practice what you put into it, so the more you do, the more you will benefit and the more your life will change as a result. As I continued my walk, I deliberately practiced. As it felt hard to inhale, I'd focus on exhaling fully.

As I did that, I found that I could easily, almost automatically take the next breath.

We need to practice releasing *everywhere* we're holding on. Is it anger? Jealousy? Resentment? Comparison? Frustration? Fear? Doubt? Insecurity? Judgment? Part of your past? What are you holding on to?

Release the way we thought it would be so we can receive what it will actually be.

We aren't letting go because we don't value what we thought it would be, but *because we do*.

We aren't releasing because we don't need it, but *because we do*.

In Practice:

Begin your practice literally. Most of us have no idea how often we aren't fully exhaling when we breathe. Take a few moments throughout the day to practice deep inhales and full exhales. Yes, it is that simple. Simple doesn't mean ineffective. In fact, it's often the opposite. Make time for it. Put it on your calendar, to-do list, or whatever tool you use for priorities.

Practice with your small annoyances or frustrations. I remember to practice every time I get annoyed on a phone call. I know, I'm sure that sounds random, but I am not much of a phone person, so the majority of times I'm on the phone it's to schedule an appointment or try to get information from a service provider of some kind. As soon as I notice my teeth clench or I recognize thoughts of *"I hate this! I wish I had someone to do this for me!"* I take several slow, complete breaths.

There are also other practices that will help, such as box breathing or Transcendental Meditation. You can Google either one of these. They're incredible options to help you relax, release, and be more intentional about what you are or aren't holding on to.

Take an inventory of things you're hanging on to: an email you got, a conversation you had, or an outburst you're still embarrassed by.

It's impossible to let go or even release a little if you don't *realize* you're hanging on to it.

Once you have an inventory of those things, decide not to be overwhelmed by it. It's not bad if you recognize you're holding on to a million things. It's not good if you can only think of a few. You are where you are; it's just data. It's a starting point.

Looking at your list, is there one you're willing to start working on?

NEGATIVE REPS

Most gym-goers are probably familiar with the term *negative rep*. In case you're not, let me take a second to get us all on the same page.

If you think about a pull-up, there are two parts to the movement: the way up and the way down. The way down is called the eccentric phase or, more simply, the negative. A push-up has the same two parts. The way down from the plank position to the floor is called the negative.

When you're trying to build strength, many trainers will have their clients work on *just* the negative portion of the rep instead of fighting to do the full movement. Some muscle groups are *only* engaged during the negative portion of the rep. A lot of strength can be built as you're going down in a slow, controlled fashion, especially when you don't yet have the strength for the full range of motion.

A couple months after my C-section with Dagny, I went

back to my local CrossFit gym. Between the significant decrease in training during my pregnancy and my recovery from abdominal surgery, my strength, stamina, and overall fitness had decreased. Pull-ups weren't yet in the cards for me, so I started to work on the negatives.

If you've seen the average person work to get their first pull-up, they fight-fight-fight to get to the top of the movement and then collapse on the way down. Unknowingly, they've lost an important opportunity to build strength. If they were to focus on control on the way down, they'd likely see improvements a lot faster.

Can you see where I'm going here? This is true in our lives, too.

When things are going well, we're focused. We're dialed in. We're paying attention and doing the work. When things start to go downhill, we often fold. We collapse. We let go of any and all structure or discipline. The hard time we're experiencing becomes the reason to disengage when it should be the very reason to remain engaged!

As I worked on my negative reps of push-ups and pull-ups— slow and controlled to build strength on the way down—I realized the opportunity to do this in my own life.

As with muscular training, there are some things you can

only improve on the way down. There are some benefits that only come when you're in the negative portion. There are skills built and strength that is only acquired when you're going down, but to take advantage of the opportunity, you have to go slow and stay controlled.

We need both. We need the way up, and we need the way down. We need the ascent *and* the decline. Our bodies need both. Our minds need both. Our faith needs both.

Practicing patience when you're frustrated will benefit you far more than practicing patience when you're calm. Practicing follow-through when you're motivated isn't going to have as much of an impact as practicing follow-through when you're not motivated. Being loving and thoughtful to my husband is wonderful when I'm in a great mood, but real strength is built and growth happens when I practice being loving and thoughtful when I'm irritated or feeling disconnected.

There is some strength that can only be developed on the way down.

Several months back I heard a bit of parenting advice that I wrote down, in hopes that I'll remember when our kids are old enough for us to apply it: provide our children with regular moments of controlled struggle to help them become resilient and capable problem solvers. I'd imagine it's also a powerful way to help them develop confidence. It reminded me of similar parenting advice I've heard regarding routine mistakes. If your child knocks over their glass of milk, instead of getting irritated or jumping up to clean it, smile and ask *"What should we do now?"* Let them seize the moment to practice problem-solving.

As I thought more about what controlled struggle might look like for a young child, I kept thinking of how powerful this same concept is for adults.

My CrossFit workouts are examples of controlled struggle. For my mental and physical fitness, it's important to expose myself to challenges that force me to rise to the occasion. My role as a business owner provides me with constant moments of controlled struggle. When my website crashes or I have to make a hard decision, these aren't barriers, they're opportunities for me to build skills and confidence that the easy moments can't provide.

I've adopted this sage parenting advice as a valuable reframe in big moments and small moments. I don't have to get annoyed by my overwhelming pregnancy craving for s'mores. It's a controlled struggle with growth advantages similar to working those negative repetitions! I don't have to have a mini breakdown when my computer crashes and I lose three hours of work. There are some skills I can only build in moments of frustration. This is a controlled struggle.

We are going to face hard moments. We are going to come up against challenges we'd rather avoid. As we do, let's remember that we need the ups *and* the downs, and often the downs hold the potential for far more growth and improvement than the ups ever will.

Capitalize on your negative reps. Choose to see them as opportunities, welcome or not, to grow and improve in ways that you can't when everything is going well.

In Practice:

With a blank journal or notebook, make a list of some of the hard times in your life. What were they? They can be huge losses, like the loss of a loved one, or they can be seasons where you struggled financially, went through a breakup, or anything in between.

What did each hard time teach you? Were there ways that you grew as a person or came out stronger?

Are you in a hard time now? Have there been any lessons or breakthroughs you've experienced?

Are there any breakthroughs or lessons you *hope* to experience?

This practice is not limited to reflection or struggle. When you're experiencing even the smallest frustration or annoyance—you're stuck in traffic, you lose your car keys, or you get a rude email—ask yourself, *"Is there a lesson in this for me? What is it? Can I use this moment to get a little better?"*

What would it look like for you to slow down and practice more control in the negatives of your life? Don't limit yourself to the big negatives, like grief or depression; think, too, about the little challenges that come in your marriage, parenting, finances, self-talk, or career.

How can you give yourself an opportunity to thrive in controlled struggle? Is there an opportunity to capitalize on controlled struggle today?

What perspective would you need to see frustrations or barriers as opportunities to challenge yourself via controlled struggle?

REGULATING OR REACTING

In 1954, Dr. Martin Luther King, Jr. gave a sermon titled "Transformed Nonconformist." In his sermon, King declared, *"The Christian is called upon not to be like a thermometer conforming to the temperature of his society but he must be like a thermostat serving to transform the temperature of his society."*

Can you recognize moments where you've conformed to the temperature around you? It could have been joining in with a group of friends who are gossiping or complaining. It could have been a time when your spouse came home angry about work and you got angry along with them. I know I have conformed to the patterns of people around me!

We always have a choice to either be the thermostat (regulator) or the thermometer (reactor).

Thinking in these terms of regulator versus reactor has been tremendously helpful in my hardest moments of grief. When spontaneous thoughts arise of my final moments with Dagny or of hurtful events in the aftermath of her death, I get to choose if I want to regulate or if I want to react. I get to choose if I'm going to conform to the thoughts or transform them. I choose if I want to stay with those thoughts and let them drive my emotional state, or if I will choose the emotional state I *want* and craft my thoughts accordingly.

It's always a choice. It's forever a practice. We don't need to conform to the temperature of our feelings. We can *set* the temperature we desire. It's about being proactive instead of reactive.

I like to think about it this way: Will I lead, or will I follow? Will I lead my mind, or will I follow it? Will I lead my thoughts, or will I follow them?

There have been many days when I wake up feeling down, discouraged, or fearful. There are times when I let that feeling reign and act as my thermostat, regulating the temperature for the day and setting the tone for my thoughts. Friend, we have other options. We don't have to follow the tone of our mood or feelings. Knowing that is step one, and it's an important step. We can choose to be the thermostat, regardless of the emotional temperature.

About six months after Dagny died, our thermostat did too (literally). We had it set on automatic so it would switch between heat and air conditioning depending on if it needed to cool things down or heat things up. We had it set to sixty-eight degrees Fahrenheit. If it worked properly, when it hit sixty-nine, the AC would kick on to cool things down a bit, but it didn't. The heat stayed on, and the temperature kept climbing. When I came into the house and it was a stuffy seventy-eight degrees, I knew something wasn't working.

This same thing happens in our own minds. Because we aren't functioning as the thermostat, when things start to get dark, fearful, and anxious, we roll with it, allowing our thoughts, words, actions, and inactions to make things even more dark, even more fearful, or even more anxious.

When we're functioning properly as the thermostat, if we're set for calm and grateful, as soon as things start to get dark, we kick in as a counter-regulatory function to change the vibe.

That counter-regulatory function is **you**. It is your thoughts and your perspectives.

Recently, this has been the most helpful for me to practice when I'm feeling angry. I don't *want* to feel angry. I hate the feeling and it's not the emotional energy I want in my home, but I've experienced a lot of anger around things that happened after Dagny died. I applied this "thermostat" practice to those moments when anger shows up.

My thermostat is set to "grateful and good," so when I notice the temperature rising in response to anger, I tell myself that's when gratitude and a focus on what's been good need to kick in. That's when *I* need to kick in as a counter-regulatory function through my thoughts and perspective.

If that thermostat *doesn't* kick in, I follow the rabbit hole of anger and the feelings intensify. The heat of anger rises because I didn't *choose* to implement my counter-regulatory capabilities.

This doesn't mean I'm not angry or that my feelings aren't valid—I am and they are. But it's not the emotional temperature I want in my life. I don't have to stay there. I don't choose to stay there. I want to practice being the regulator and not the reactor.

We get to make this a practice. I promise, the universe will give you thousands of chances to practice. It's a tool, but as with all tools, it only has utility when you use it. Will you fuel the fire of emotion, or will you cool it down?

Show up as your own thermostat. Make it a practice. You

have to engage deliberately. You have to kick on. You have to do the work with awareness and countermeasures.

You have to do it even if you don't want to. I imagine the thermostat would often rather rest. It often doesn't care if we overheat, but it has a job to do, and so do you.

In Practice:

What do you want your emotional thermostat set to? What do you want it set to in your marriage? What do you want it set to in your career? Look at this for each area of your life.

When you notice your temperature rising, what can you do to cool things down?

When you notice your emotional temperature dropping, what might you do to raise it?

What are the kinds of things that set you off or fire you up? Get familiar with a list of things that push your buttons. How can you shift your response to them so your temperature doesn't rise? What way of thinking would you need to have in order not to react?

Every time you notice your temperature rising, this is your opportunity to practice. You have to *desire* this change.

Remember, sometimes, out of sheer stubbornness, we want to be mad. We want to stay mad. We want to justify why we are mad. But is that really how you want to live?

Enlist your family. Have this discussion together and brainstorm ways to kick in as the thermostat.

RIDE OR DRIVE

In the early months after Dagny's death, I had this low-level fear that I would lose everything I had worked so hard for. I thought the business I had worked so hard to build, the health habits I had fought hard to establish, the financial security I had created for our family...I thought it would slowly disappear while I stumbled through the dark halls of grief.

For most of my life, I tried to escape stress, pain, loss, or any adversity. I have a long history of telling myself that food or mindless television would soothe me. I used food as an anesthetic for decades and, relatively speaking, don't have as much experience coping with big pain in healthy ways.

Now, facing the most agonizing period in my life, I didn't feel confident in my ability to navigate this without those learned crutches. Sure, my experience with coping in destructive ways gave me the intellectual understanding that avoiding isn't the same as resolving and that turning to food or television only created additional suffering, but it *didn't* give me the tools to live through this loss in a healthy way. I knew what *didn't* work, but I didn't know what did.

I had no desire to "get over it," which worked in my favor. I didn't want to forget. I didn't even want the pain to go away because that felt like forgetting or dismissing just how much I loved Dagny. My goal became finding a way to take care of myself while allowing for the pain of loss to be as big and as present as it needed to be.

In the last year, I've had a lot of practice not running away from hard and uncomfortable feelings. **So much of our impulse behavior comes from an unwillingness to stay with an uncomfortable feeling.** However, running away isn't real. It's not possible. We can't leave the feelings behind. They're still there waiting for us while we distract or numb.

When I feel like a wave of grief is too strong to survive, I just need to make more space for it. The struggle often comes more from resistance to the feeling than from the feeling itself.

It reminds me of how I approached contractions while laboring. If you fight against them and tense your body, you make the pain worse. You have to make space for it. Relax your body; relax your mind; let it go through you, uncontested. It's not easy, but it is possible. So it is with emotional pain. Stop running from it; you're making it worse.

The idea that food, television, drugs, alcohol, spending money, or anything else is an escape...these are false promises.

I learned a new way to respond to strong emotions and painful circumstances by reminding myself that the story of how I feel isn't relevant to the reality of what I choose.

Over and over I tell myself that **this feeling can ride with me, but it cannot drive**.

I distinctly remember an afternoon when I had work that needed to be done but I had zero desire to do any of it. I had a meeting to get on, and I just didn't care. I thought, *"I just want to stay here on the couch and eat Cheez-Its and ice cream."*

I used the moment to coach myself. This grief can ride with me, but it cannot drive. The grief can come with me to this meeting, but it can't make decisions for me. **Grief doesn't decide what I eat.**

We can separate what we feel from what we do. It's a practice. I can be angry *and* respond with kindness. I can be annoyed *and* show grace. I can be sad *and* make a healthy choice. So can you.

Recently I had a week that brought a lot of challenges. In addition to grief and isolation there were autopsy results, hard questions, gross weather, relationship tension, medical bills, emotional conversations, and traumatic nightmares. With every choice that followed these circumstances, I got to practice, again and again, that the story of how I feel isn't relevant to the reality of what I choose.

I can feel unmotivated and go for a walk.

I can feel apathetic and cook a healthy meal.

I can be hurt and communicate with kindness.

For the first thirty years of my life, feelings and choices were *one tangled mess of immature cause and effect*. The way I felt in the moment influenced my choices. That's an extremely unpredictable way to live, linking your choices to the emotional state of the moment.

Don't get me wrong: feelings matter—mine and yours. I'm giving myself a ton of space to feel it all. The difference is: my choices remain separate and don't have to be controlled by my emotional weather.

We save so much time and energy when we don't use our feelings as context or prelude to our choices.

We can avoid wild inconsistency by not making what we choose about how we feel.

We're often quicker to notice this behavior in others than we are to see it in ourselves. It's easy to recognize when a friend bails on your workout because she's had a stressful day or when your spouse suggests pizza because he's exhausted. The most power comes when we look for this way of thinking in *ourselves* and practice choosing another way.

The feeling can ride with you, but it doesn't have to drive.

We named our daughter Dagny after the lead character Dagny Taggart in Ayn Rand's classic novel *Atlas Shrugged*. I have so many favorite quotes from the book, and there's one in particular that I wrestled with for a while. I didn't know if I liked it or totally disagreed with it. In the book, Dagny says, *"Do it first. Feel about it later."*

When I first read those words, I thought they were justifying something like being rude and feeling bad about it later or eating the ice cream and regretting it afterwards.

In grief, I understand this quote very differently.

My feelings don't have to block my actions.

I don't have to deny my feelings or judge them, but I also don't have to let them drive my actions or inactions.

I can choose to just do it.

I can choose to put aside how I feel and deal with that after.

Do it first. Feel about it afterwards.

I thought about this last night as I sat on the couch watching *Shark Tank* and putting off the dishes. *"I don't feel like getting up to do the dishes,"* I thought.

That's exactly what this quote is about. Do it first. Feel about it afterwards.

I don't have to feel like it. **That's not even relevant unless I make it relevant.**

I don't feel like apologizing.

Well, I don't have to feel like it and neither do you. Do it first, feel about it afterwards.

Stop letting your feelings block the straight path to action.

In Practice:

Pay attention as you're making choices. Pay attention to big choices and small—what you choose to eat or not eat, if you choose to work out or not, how you respond to a loved one when you're feeling angry or frustrated.

What feelings are you allowing to factor into the choice you're considering?

If you were to remove how you feel, or if you were to feel quite differently, what choice might you make?

Objectively speaking, without any emotion factoring in, what is the best decision or the decision that reflects who or how you want to be?

START BEFORE YOU'RE READY

Many years ago, still weighing over 300 pounds, I decided to join a CrossFit gym. I had never done CrossFit, and it flat-out terrified me. But I had a burning desire to be fit and healthy, so I started looking up gyms near me to see if any of them offered one-on-one coaching.

The majority of CrossFit gyms exclusively offer group classes, and at the time I wasn't willing to begin such a journey in front of a bunch of strangers. I found a Cross-Fit gym in my town where one of the owners would work individually with me before the gym opened, and I dove in before I could talk myself out of it.

My new trainer, Nathan, and I hit it off. I adored him, and he provided me with a healthy balance of encouragement, understanding, and high expectations.

Most CrossFit workouts are high intensity, and I found myself pausing frequently to catch my breath between repetitions of new-to-me moves like box jumps, burpees, and wall balls. In every workout, Nathan would cue me in the most helpful way while I took that tired, hesitant pause: *start before you're ready.*

Get back to the next rep before you're ready.

Pick up that barbell before you're ready.

Start on your next sprint before you're ready.

Time after time, his reminder to start before I was ready got me back into action before I felt like it. Without his cue, I probably would have taken anywhere from a few more seconds to half a minute before diving back in. In some cases, without his reminder, I might have stopped altogether because that sense of "ready" would never have come.

His advice made me fitter. It made me bolder. It helped my confidence grow because I could actually do a lot more than my doubtful mind imagined.

After hearing that cue week in and week out, it started to stick. One night, I couldn't help but laugh as I sat on the couch, putting off an evening chore, when his words popped into my mind: start before you're ready.

I didn't feel like getting up to put away my mountain of laundry, and I certainly didn't want to step away from my television show, but I knew I didn't have to wait until I felt ready.

I began using his cue all over the place. When my alarm went off in the morning and I felt far from ready to get up, I'd tell myself to start before I was ready. When I recognized that I was avoiding the start of a new task at work, I'd cue myself to start before I was ready. Even when I knew I needed to apologize to my husband but I didn't want to yet, I'd remind myself to start before I was ready.

It wasn't long before Nathan's words felt like my own and I was using them more often outside the gym than inside it.

Not surprisingly, it remained a go-to tool in my grief. The very day after Dagny died, Chris and I had to drive to New Hampshire for a meeting at the funeral home. We had an early morning appointment, and I was far from ready to get dressed and out the door. My breasts were tender and full of milk, and I still looked and felt pregnant. I definitely wasn't ready to talk about our daughter's funeral arrangements. I hadn't yet even accepted the fact that she was gone!

I stared blankly at the wall, feeling utterly incapable of getting dressed, when Nathan's coaching came to mind: start before you're ready. I could have sat on that bed for the rest of my life and never felt ready for the discussion we were about to have, but I didn't have to wait to feel ready. I knew the value of starting before I was ready.

Reluctantly, I put my clothes on and headed to the car.

As the weeks pressed on, I continued to be faced with things I wasn't ready to do. I wasn't ready to see my obstetrician for my postoperative follow-up. She didn't even know that Dagny had died. I wasn't ready deliver Dagny's eulogy. I wasn't ready for my first workout or to get on video with my clients. Each time, I started before I was ready.

This tool shouldn't be reserved for heavy things like meetings with funeral directors or delivering eulogies. I still use it during my workouts. It helps me when I don't feel like cleaning the kitchen or getting ready for bed. It helps me when I am not in the mood to write or when the last thing I feel like doing is responding to my accountant's email full of questions.

Look for places where you're procrastinating. Every moment of delay is a chance to practice. Turn off the television and go up to bed before you feel ready. Clean up the kitchen before you're ready. Speak with love and patience to your kids before your annoyance or frustration has worn off. Start the project, begin your workout, or make your next healthy choice, and do it before you feel ready.

In Practice:

Where do you find yourself in a pattern of delay or procrastination?

In what area of your life would you benefit most from getting into action more quickly?

Just one time, are you able and willing to start before you're ready?

Can you find three opportunities today to start before you're ready?

Where can you put this reminder to help you identify opportunities each day to put it into practice?

FLYERS FLY

Have you ever seen a trapeze show? Recently, I heard someone talk about how trapeze artists train. Typically, you have one person flying through the air on a small bar and another person swinging from a similar device, and one catches the other. Apparently, as a trapeze artist, you're either a designated flyer or a designated catcher. The flyer is the one who has to let go and connect to the catcher.

One of the first and most important things the flyer learns is that their job is to fly. Their job is *not* to catch. If the flyer tries to catch the catcher, they're both likely to get hurt. Let the flyer fly; let the catcher catch. The flyer only needs to focus on flying well. The catcher will take care of the catching.

In the first few months after Dagny died, I worked to do so much more than my job. I tried to make the people closest to me understand how I felt (not my job). I tried to make Chris talk about his feelings (not my job either). I wanted to figure out every little thing that could have or should have gone differently. I wondered how we could continue on and have a family.

This lesson from the trapeze artists reminded me that my job is just to fly. My job is to do my part as well as I possibly can.

When I started thinking about it this way, I realized just how often I limited my own role by trying to take on the roles of others. Instead of focusing on improving my own communication, I tried to improve Chris's, too. Years ago, I did this with my first husband. Instead of staying in my own lane and focusing on improving my own health, I took on the responsibility of trying to improve his health, too.

I see similar patterns with my clients. I hosted a webinar recently, and someone asked this related question: *"I've been doing a ton of mindset work and really getting better about being in the present and not getting stuck in the past or the future. It's been amazing. My family is totally not this way. How do I get them on board with this new way of thinking?"*

You don't.

You can't do your job and their job. Your job is to fly. Your job is you.

I tell people this all the time when they ask about how they can convince their loved ones to eat better or start working out. You can't. I advise them to think of it as being a lighthouse—be a light so bright that others are drawn to you. You focus on living as well as you can, on being as healthy as you can, on being as happy as you can, and others will be drawn to you and your example.

It's easy to pretend that we don't know our part just as it's easy to get lost in thinking that other people's parts are our responsibility.

There's a quote from James Wedmore that always helps me focus on my part. He says, *"People dream of cake. Then life gives them batter, eggs, oil, icing, pan, oven...they get frustrated and leave the kitchen. Sometimes you have everything right there in front of you, you just have to take the action to make it happen."*

Though I've seen it many times before, it hit me differently after Dagny died. As I often do, I asked myself, *"How does this apply to me right now? How can I use this right now?"*

Initially, I felt frustrated. What I want, my dream, is to have Dagny back. I can't. I don't have the ingredients for that. I can't make it happen.

If I let the initial emotionally charged response settle and I wait patiently for the next wave of thought, I realize there are *other* things I want, too.

I want a big, healthy family. I want to be pregnant again. I believe God put that desire in my heart immediately to help me heal and give me hope.

Sure, I can't make my cycle return and I can't inseminate myself, but there are other ingredients for this "cake" of a big, healthy family. I don't want to stop at wanting Dagny back and being devastated that she's gone. As hard as it is, there are more ingredients to my desire. There's more possibility than I initially considered.

A strong relationship

A healthy body

A happy home

Financial stability

These are things I can take action on. I have a role to play in each of these pursuits. That's enough to focus on without saddling myself with other people's work, other people's mindsets or choices. Sure, it's not easy, but why do we need it to be easy when it's worth it?

When I work with clients, I help them focus on *today* instead of on the big picture. The focus of a strong relationship can feel quite ambiguous from a long-term view. I don't control my partner, and I don't know how to make things better.

But when we ask ourselves what we can do today to make our relationship stronger, it feels easier to answer.

You can be kind.

You can say nothing when you want to be rude or short-tempered.

You can be warm instead of distant.

You can offer a compliment.

When I consider what I can do *today* to make my body more healthy, the answer feels clear.

I can drink plenty of water.

I can avoid sugar and processed foods.

I can take a long walk.

I can do one more push-up.

I can take my supplements.

I can eat real, clean foods and lots of veggies.

I can do these things, whether I want to or not, because my "cake" is a big, healthy family.

My part.

There's so much I can't control. I can't bring Dagny back. I can't control whether or not we get answers as to how she died. I can't control other people. I can't control the depth of grief.

The other night, I asked myself if I'm controlling and optimizing the things I can. As I see it, the most important thing I can control is how I care for my body and my mind.

I can contribute to the problem, the grief, the isolation, the sadness, and the depression by overeating or eating poorly. That will make it worse for me both emotionally and physically.

Alternatively, I can contribute to the solution. I can increase my emotional bandwidth and support the production of feel-good neurotransmitters by eating well and meditating. I can help my body and my mind heal from physical and emotional trauma by eating well, staying hydrated, exercising, and meditating.

Are you optimizing the things you can? Do you have clarity on what those things are?

We always have a part in the solution, whether or not we choose to play it.

We can also always have a part in the problem, too. We can compound it, knowingly or unknowingly.

The problem is big and ugly enough all on its own. The last thing I want to do is anything that will make it worse. Our problems are big enough for us to focus on. We don't need to add the weight of someone else's journey. Do your part and only your part.

In Practice:

Are you optimizing the things you can? Do you have clarity on what those things are?

What is your role in the dream you have for yourself?

What ingredients are available to you?

Where are you trying to do your part and someone else's?

What does it look like to leave their part to them?

What aspects of your part will you capitalize on today?

NOW OR READY?

During my daily walks, I've been telling God how hard this season has been and more or less begging for a new season. I've been hoping for a new season and feeling like I need a new season.

Once again, a mindset upgrade came to me via an Elevation Church sermon. The pastor shared that God is less concerned with moving me into a new season **now** than He is with moving me into a new season **ready**.

I don't know about you, but often, I want it *now*. I rarely am okay with the waiting or preparing.

When I think back to when I weighed over 350 pounds, I wanted nothing more than to be fit and lean. I wanted it now. I hated the notion of how long it would take to lose as much weight as I wanted to. I would have done just about anything to snap my fingers and magically be in my ideal body. However, I wasn't ready. I hadn't changed my behaviors. I hadn't changed the way I thought about food or fitness. I wanted it now, but it would have done nothing for me if I didn't arrive ready.

I wanted to be pregnant again immediately and felt like it couldn't happen soon enough—an annoyingly similar situation. I wanted it now, but I had to be ready. My body had to be ready, and my mind had to be ready.

I didn't necessarily love or welcome this new perspective, but I do agree with it. I thought about my body, still recovering from pregnancy and C-section. I thought about my heart, still heavy with grief. I couldn't control if or when I would get pregnant, but I could control the extent to which I was ready mentally, physically, emotionally, and financially.

This mindset shift moved me from a desperate pleading to conceive to an eager sense of responsibility to ready myself. Each day, and often with each choice, I'd consider what I could do to be ready. My steps were never dramatic, but it's this way of thinking that shifted me out of *"I don't care"* thoughts and into *"I want to be ready"* thoughts.

I got more consistent with workouts.

I fueled my body more intelligently.

I started prioritizing sleep and seeing a chiropractor, an acupuncturist, and a massage therapist.

If you aren't where you want to be yet, if you're in a season that feels hard, it might be that you need to be more **ready** before the season changes.

Feeling ready isn't the same as being ready.

Maybe your attitude needs to be more ready.

Maybe your habits need to be more ready.

Maybe your perspective isn't ready.

Consider, each day, how you can become ready.

In Practice:

What is it that you want?

If you were observing a person who is/has what you want, what might they do today that is different from your own choices or habits?

Which of those things are you willing to do today?

What perspective would you need to have to approach whatever new chapter you desire with an eager sense of responsibility to ready yourself?

What's the difference between feeling ready and *being* ready?

Create a habit of asking these questions every day, for months.

What is it that you need to be ready for?

What does it mean to be ready?

Consider these questions for your health, family, finances, relationship, career, friendships, fitness, and any other area of your life that matters to you.

What will you do today to ready yourself for the next season of your life?

CREATE A CLEAR LENS

I've been wearing contact lenses since the second grade. I wore glasses for less than a year before deciding I was old enough for contact lenses. My mom made a rule: if I wanted to wear contacts, I had to take care of them myself. Though I was only seven years old, that meant I had to put them in by myself, take them out by myself, and care for them properly. If I couldn't do that, I had to keep wearing glasses.

I'll never forget my first night with my new contacts. My mom had gone out for the evening, and my older sister and I were home alone at bedtime. I panicked at the thought of taking out my contacts all by myself. I didn't want to admit to my mom that I couldn't do it, as that would have meant continuing to wear my big glasses! After a lot of tears (which only make it harder to remove contacts), I finally got them out, and the rest is history.

If you've ever been to an eye doctor to establish your prescription for glasses or contacts, you've likely had the memorable experience of flipping back and forth between what seems like a million options as you look through the black occluder that hangs in front of the exam chair.

"Is this one better? How about this one? Can you see more clearly here? Or here? How about this one? Is it better like this or like this?"

I often get flustered in those appointments because I can't seem to remember the first option by the time they've switched to the second one, but even if you have to toggle back and forth a dozen times, *there is always something that is more clear.*

The same is true in life.

There is usually a more or most clear perspective, we just don't always give ourselves multiple options. Shortly after Dagny died, I started asking myself a series of questions to help me identify a better perspective or choice.

Through which lens is the choice clear?

Which perspective feels better?

What perspective or outlook do I need to have in order for this choice to be clear?

This practice of mine started around food and self-care choices. I had a hard time doing *anything*. I didn't want to eat, didn't want to go outside, didn't want to talk to anyone, didn't want to get groceries or go to the gym. The answer to almost every question I asked myself: *"I don't care."* I knew that could quickly become a slippery slope if I let it!

Similar to my eye exam, everything was blurry when I looked through the lens of *"Dagny has died, and nothing matters now."* Everything was gray.

But I knew that wasn't the *only* lens, even if it was the only one I looked through. I *can* look through that lens, I can choose that lens and I often do, but it's not the *only* lens. The world looks a certain way through that lens, but that doesn't mean the world *is* that way or that there isn't more to see and consider.

While switching back and forth between different perspectives, I started asking, *"Is it more clear like this? How about this? Can I see better now?"*

For example, if I switched to the lens of *"I want a big family. Chris and I want to have many more kids,"* certain things became more clear.

If I should work out or not became more clear. If I should

cook breakfast or not, what I should cook for breakfast—those things became more clear.

Sometimes I'd be looking through the lens of *"Work doesn't matter anymore. Nothing matters without Dagny,"* and that would make it difficult to get into my email inbox or draft a social media post.

So I'd step back and ask myself, *"Through which lens is this more clear?"*

Things became more clear through the lens of, *"This work matters. This work allows me to build a home and care for the family I desire. So many people are working through similar pain, and I can help them if I share."*

I feel hurt when I look through this lens: *"They didn't even bother to call one single time after hearing our daughter died. All the times I was there for them and they couldn't even call me."* Just like all the lenses at the eye doctor are real, they aren't all helpful. They aren't all best. Same here. These lenses are real, they're not most helpful, and they aren't best when I'm trying to see more clearly.

I'd ask myself, *"Through which lens am I less angry or hurt?"*

I'd think about our Cape friends who drove hours and then stood in the parking lot for hours until we were ready to leave. I think about the people who did wrap their arms around us, literally, and gave us the exact thing we needed. I think about all the people who still talk about Dagny, months later, and genuinely care about how we're doing.

There's always another lens. This is a tool we can all practice daily.

Maybe you want to fire off an aggressive text message through the lens of *"Are you kidding me? How selfish of her!"* But is it more clear when you look at it a different way, through a different lens?

How would you have to look at it to see things differently?

I use this a lot with food.

When considering dinner options with a perspective of *"I'm stressed and tired,"* calling for pizza to be delivered seems like a very reasonable and appealing choice. But, if I choose a different perspective, everything looks different.

When I look through the lens of *"I want to be a positive and powerful example for my children and I want to be in the habit of modeling healthy choices,"* it certainly looks different. It looks more clear. There are always so many options and perspectives we can filter through. I think about who I want to be, who I used to be and how that felt, the kind of behavior I want to model for my children, how I will feel a day or two after making different choices, what I might choose if people I admire were with me, and so much more.

This is a great tool for money, as well. When I look through the lens of how good it would feel to buy a new set of pots and pans and the fact that I can afford it, the choice seems clear.

As always, there are other lenses.

It looks very different through the lens that reminds me I have completely functional pots and pans and spending $1,000 to have them match is a little silly, when the only time I'd notice they match is when I open the cabinet since I rarely cook with more than one pot at a time.

This practice has helped me avoid thousands of fights with my husband. There's always a lens that makes me angry or makes me feel not considered or not prioritized. But there are always other lenses.

No eye doctor would give you just one option for your glasses. Never give yourself just one option for your behavior or response.

If you see lack, look again. If you see anger, look again. If you see pain, look again. Try on a new perspective.

Leadership and personal development author Jim Collins writes about the genius of the word "and" and the tyranny of the word "or."

The word "and" reminds us that we aren't wrong in our first perspective, there are simply additional options. The word "and" expands our thinking, our options, and our potential.

The word "or" makes us think we have to choose, but we don't.

It's not either this perspective or that one. It's this perspective *and* that one. It's this reality *and* that one. It's this option *and* that one.

The word "or" can be tyrannical while the word "and" is expansive. Remember: the goal isn't to find the *right* perspective but rather to invite *more* perspectives.

For example, I'm pretty sure it's human nature to initially see things as happening *to* you. If you lose your job, though you might ultimately come to see it as a huge blessing, your first instinct is likely not as rosy.

If your spouse cheats, you get audited by the IRS, or you lose a loved one, there's a valid argument that these things happened *to* you. You didn't ask for it, you didn't cause it, and it might have been 100 percent outside of your control.

One day while I walked along the canal, I wondered, *"Is there a difference between what is happening to me and what is happening through me? Should there be? Could there be? What's the difference between what is happening to me and what is happening in me?"*

I didn't ask to shift my attention away from the loss I navigated. I didn't want to rewrite my perspective on how devastating it was to watch my daughter die. I didn't argue that it didn't happen to me. I just wanted to evaluate whether or not there was, or could be, more going on inside me. I attempted to round out the full picture. **I wanted to see additional perspectives, not as a replacement of my original point of view, but in addition to it.**

What was happening *in* me?

I was getting closer to God every day. I was questioning, challenging, and reconsidering what I do and don't want for my life. I was identifying survival tools and writing them down to share with others who are struggling. I was being called to slow down, simplify, and re-evaluate my work.

What was happening *through* me?

This book, for one. Even before I crafted these pages, the bits I shared through my Daily Mindset Upgrades or on social media encouraged and supported people.

Sometimes, we miss the gift or the opportunity because we're exclusively focused on what's happening *to* us. We're focused on one sharp perspective.

There's always more to see, we just have to remember to look.

In Practice:

Create a habit of asking yourself, *"Through which lens is the choice most clear?"*

Through which lens do you have to look to feel peaceful, calm, happy, grateful, hopeful, or content?

Through which lens do you have to look to feel motivated or determined?

What perspective would you need to have to feel _____?

Keep in mind that you don't have to choose any or every one of these perspectives, just like you don't have to choose any or every one of the lenses displayed through the occluder at the doctor's office. You're just trying them on.

The more perspectives you try on, the more likely you will be to clearly see which one works best for the moment you're in.

TO CATCH A FISH

One morning, I made it to the canal for my walk fairly early. By 6:30 a.m., fishermen already dotted the path along the canal. If you didn't know, fishing is a fairly complex hobby. These early risers had to dress for it, gather all their gear, pack it all up, drive to the canal, and then bike a mile or so to get to their fishing spot. That's all *before* the fishing even begins!

As I started off on my walk, I thought about these fishermen. All that time spent in preparation doesn't matter. It's not enough to get them what they want: a haul of fish. In fact, none of the preparation gets them a single fish.

They won't catch fish because they woke up early.

They won't catch fish because they're at the water's edge.

They won't catch fish because they have bait.

They won't catch fish because they have a pole.

They won't catch fish because they rode their bikes to a hot spot.

They only catch fish when they do what it takes, and it takes more than preparation.

As I thought about it, I had to ask myself, *"Am I doing what it takes to get the results I want, or do I just look like it? Am I doing what it takes to get the results I want, or am I just prepped and ready?"*

Are you doing what it takes to get results, or does it just look like it?

Reading the relationship book doesn't improve your relationship. Showing up differently does. Changing your behavior and upgrading your responses improves your relationship. Are you listening to podcasts, buying cookbooks, and planning how much you'll weigh if you lose two pounds per week between now and the next major holiday?

Even though it might look like it, that's not doing what it takes.

Do you have a Peloton bike and a few hundred bucks' worth of new leggings and sports bras? Are you trying to be fit, or does it just look like it? Are you getting out of debt, or does it just look like it? Do you read the books, make the plans, and then fail to follow them? Are you doing what it takes to get results in your business, or do you just look like it?

Having a plan and the intent to execute won't get it done any more than knowing which pole to use will catch a fish.

I continue to ask myself, *"Am I doing what it takes to be healthier and support my body's ability to bear children for many, many more years? Or do I just look like it?"*

Some people will get frustrated when they realize they just look the part but aren't doing what it takes. I'm not trying to call you out, I'm merely asking you to get curious about if you're doing what it takes to get results. When I get frustrated with my behavior or my results, I remind myself to get curious instead of critical.

If you aren't yet consistently doing what it takes to get results, that's okay. Every single choice is a chance to make that change today.

In Practice:

Instead of, *"Oh my God, that's so me. I just look the part, and I'm not doing what it takes!"* I'd suggest you ask questions, like:

What's the difference between doing what it takes (for your specific goal) and just looking like it?

What can you do today to get the results you want?

What can you implement that you already know but aren't yet consistently doing?

What would you need to do to get the results you want?

Of those things you identified, which of them will you do today?

SELECTING A SEASON

Before I go to bed each night, I turn off Wi-Fi on my phone. When I'm recording a podcast or on a live webinar, I put my phone on airplane mode to prevent texts and calls from coming through. When I need to make or receive a call or text, I make sure I'm *not* on airplane mode. My point? Your phone has many modes, and they all serve a purpose.

This is also true in our lives, even if you operate, as most of us operate, as though there is only one mode. For years, I operated as though there was only one mode in my life: go mode.

Get better, do better, make more money, build my business, lose weight, improve my fitness. Go, go, go. I treated every day, every goal, and every obstacle the same way. Push, grind, hustle, solve.

This default mode threw me for a loop after Dagny died. I

felt unsettled by not being in go mode. It felt like the only "right" mode or the only "good enough" mode.

As I scaled back my business activities out of sheer necessity, I saw the value and power of a different mode. I felt greater clarity, I became more creative, and I suddenly had time and space to create the structure and organization that I had wanted for years.

I started to consider that maybe "go" wasn't the only mode I should live in. Maybe there's value, tremendous value, in a "slow" mode. Maybe there is an important role and time for both. Were there other modes of value I had been ignoring?

Go mode.

Slow mode.

Sow mode.

Show mode.

Where do I need to be for the needs I have at the moment?

When I'm in go mode, I want to see results. If they don't come fast enough, I try something new or buckle down and work harder.

When I am in show mode, results are manifesting. Opportunities are present. Growth and improvement are obvious.

When I'm in sow mode, I'm making investments. The returns aren't immediate, but I'm putting in the work and establishing the foundation.

Knowing what you want and need for the phase of life you're in can help you determine which mode is appropriate for your season. It's important to remember that you might be in different modes in different areas of your life at one time.

As we welcome a new baby soon, I anticipate that our marriage relationship will shift into a new mode. It won't be about eagerly investing in each other but rather allowing the other to adjust to a new season and observing how they operate within it. We will likely have fewer date nights for a while, less intimacy and less time as a couple. That's okay. It's a season. What matters most is that we're intentional about what makes that new season valuable and how we can operate within it so that we benefit from it—and of course, ensuring that it is *just* a season and not a phase we remain in indefinitely.

When I first started Primal Potential, there was a great need for sow mode, though I didn't recognize it as such at the time. I probably would have been a lot more patient with the trials if I understood the different modes of life and their value. I worked hard, trying a lot of new things, building a foundation but not reaping measurable rewards from my effort. In sow mode, the results come later.

As I prepare for this new baby, I am in go mode with my home, my finances, and writing this book. I am in slow mode in my business and sow mode in my marriage.

No, these shifts and transitions are not always comfortable or easy!

Shortly after I found out I was pregnant again only six months after Dagny was born, I remember expressing fear and concern to a mentor of mine. I feared that I would slip back into a previous version of myself, one I did not like. I wasn't as productive as I was used to being. I watched more television, slept later, worked out inconsistently, and dieted erratically.

Though I knew I was in control of all my choices, I struggled to take control.

Much of this discomfort came from the fact that I didn't realize the true need for slow mode in my work and my personal life. My hormones were all over the place at just six months postpartum and newly pregnant. My mental and emotional resources were going towards navigating grief and processing our loss of Dagny and everything that came along with it. Work shifted dramatically as a result of COVID and personnel changes.

I didn't do anything wrong. I hadn't lost my mojo. I wasn't lazy. My season had shifted, and I couldn't see the need for or the benefits of it.

Truthfully, it wasn't until I began shifting *out* of that slower mode that I recognized its value. I needed that rest and phase of less motivation and sparse execution so I would be better prepared for the season of getting things done before baby. I needed the space that came from that rest to step back and evaluate what I wanted my life to look like.

These different modes have different purposes, and we will operate best when we use the right mode at the right time.

Most of us are super clear on show mode. We're clear on the results we want and the things we want to create for our lives.

Do you have equal clarity regarding sow mode?

What's required of you in go mode?

What's required of you in slow mode?

Another way I like to think of this concept is as selecting a season.

When I shifted out of weight-loss mode for the first time in years, I felt uncomfortable. I had oversimplified things in my mind, and I believed that if I didn't lose weight, I would gain it. If weight loss wasn't the objective, what would be? If I wasn't eating to lose weight, then what? I imagine many of you are reading this thinking, *"Maintenance, duh!"* but at that time in my life, I viewed it as either on or off, and it made me nervous.

Fortunately for me, my mindset had improved quite a bit when I found out I was pregnant. I was heavier than I had been in years. I hadn't lost the baby weight from my pregnancy with Dagny and now was expecting again.

I reminded myself that while the desired outcome has changed, the process didn't necessarily need to change.

The desired outcome became maintaining my weight and growing a very healthy baby, but the process didn't need to change much at all. I could still continue to eat whole foods, emphasizing protein, fats, and veggies while minimizing starch and sugar. I didn't want the results I had wanted in previous seasons, but my process didn't need to change much at all.

As you switch seasons, consider that the process might not change much, even if the desired outcome is different. That's why we have to be deliberate and intentional.

You can be in a season of push. You can be in a season of patience. The desired outcome is likely very different, but the process might not change much at all.

Progress doesn't necessarily mean go mode.

Progress can come from rest.

Progress can come from patience.

Progress can come from stepping back and changing your desired outcome.

Incredible things can come from a new approach, a new perspective, a little space, or a mindset upgrade.

In Practice:

You don't need to know the season you're in in every area of your life. You can focus on just one area, especially if this is new to you. In your self-care, what season do you need to be in? What might that look like? Or, if self-care isn't a top priority, answer these questions of your marriage, your finances, your career, or your role in your home.

Based on what you want and need most, what mode would be most valuable to you, and what will that look like today?

Does the desired outcome need to change? Does the process need to change? Does the perspective need to change? How?

Put a process in place to check your mode often and adjust as needed.

YOU ARE THE ANCHOR

In the last year, I've had a myriad of fearful thoughts. I've manufactured fear with thoughts that I might not ever get pregnant again. I've manufactured fear with thoughts that something awful will happen to this baby I'm presently carrying. I've manufactured fear with thoughts that my business will collapse due to the changes I'm making. I've manufactured fear with thoughts of loss, lack, and limitation.

These fears all reflect low-level beliefs.

For years, I've told myself and my clients that we are not our thoughts; we are the thinkers of the thoughts. **We have final say over where we allow our attention to rest.** What we choose to do with our attention has a massive impact on how we feel and the choices that shape our lives.

Undoubtedly, stressful or anxious thoughts will spontaneously arise, but we're in control of whether or not we stay there.

In the twenty-four-hour news cycle surrounding the COVID-19 pandemic, many of us have become headline readers more than truth seekers. Headlines, summaries, and short clips are everywhere, and people grab these snippets and call them truth.

Regrettably, we do this *most* in our own lives.

"I'm stuck," "I can't," and *"I always"* are headlines. They're sensational, dramatic, and wildly incomplete. When we say or think these kinds of thoughts, we've opted out of the entire story in favor of an emotional (and limiting) soundbite.

As I navigated the early months of my grief, I did the same thing with headlines like, *"I can't do this."* I'd grab that headline in my own mind and run with it, letting it lead me down a path of hopelessness and despair. It was sensational, dramatic, and yes, incomplete. There was, and is, so much more to the story.

I looked at one painful thread and called it the completed piece, but it wasn't. The headline isn't the whole story, but I allowed my attention to lock in on it.

The thoughts we choose to fuel with our attention have a significant, and often immediate, impact on how our bodies physically function. Your thoughts impact what your body is *doing*.

Think about this familiar scenario. You're tucked into bed at night and suddenly hear an unexpected noise downstairs. Slightly panicked, you think, *"Is someone in the house?!"* Sure, it starts as *just* a thought, but your brain responds to your thoughts by producing and releasing chemicals that match the type of thought you had. When you have that thought of fear or alarm, your brain responds by producing adrenaline and other stress hormones. That's why, just as quickly as you had the thought, your body begins to *feel* in a way that matches the thought. Your heart rate increases. You start breathing a little faster. Your brain has produced and released chemicals to match the thought, which prompts you to think more thoughts that match those feelings. *"Should I get up and look? What would I do if there's an intruder in here?!"* Once again, your brain responds to your thoughts by producing more chemicals to match the thoughts, and the cycle continues. What started as exclusively mental quickly becomes physical. Your body gets involved with your thoughts every single time.

When you fuel low-level beliefs with your attention, you're not only selling yourself a limiting headline, you're also anchoring your body to a feeling that is created by those thoughts. **That physical state of worry, anxiety, fear, or doubt can become your comfort zone when you spend considerable time there.** *These thoughts and feelings you create become the filter through which you consider and ultimately make your choices.*

You know who else shares headlines without depth or complete truth?

Newscasters. What else are those newscasters called?

If you guessed anchors, you're right! Do you see the power in that title?

They anchor the listener to the headline.

They set the tone, and often, they set *your* tone.

Even if you aren't a news watcher, you are the anchor in your own life. You anchor yourself to the headline news you're telling yourself about your life, your past, your future, and your circumstances.

I'm so exhausted.

I can't get ahead.

I'm a mess.

Guess what? There's a lot more to your story than that. Moreover, that's a crappy headline to anchor yourself to!

You don't have to put your problem at the center of your story.

You don't have to put your trouble as the headline of your narrative.

I don't have enough time.

I don't know what to do.

My team isn't good enough.

My spouse isn't on the same page.

I'm an emotional eater.

Remove the problem from the center of the story.

Stop telling yourself a piece of the narrative and calling it the truth.

The limit

The fear

The doubt

The past

The problem

You're the headline creator in your life. You are the anchor. You decide if you're focused on the problem or the solution. You choose whether to connect with the problem or with possibility. You can hold yourself to the standard of telling the whole story.

Do you hate media sensationalizing as much as I do? The thing is, we're doing it with our own thoughts and stories on a regular basis! We do it every time we oversimplify, every time we overdramatize, and every time we focus on a headline without the whole story.

Stop endorsing and rehearsing low-level beliefs and partial truths that only reflect the limitation.

Here are some questions I ask myself when I recognize these patterns I want to change:

How can I put my potential at the center of the story?

How can I put my goal at the center of the story?

How can I put my power at the center of the story?

What would it look like if I focused only on my potential or possibility?

How can I tell a story that reflects where I'm going and what I want instead of where I've been and what I don't want?

What am I leaving out?

Make space for new thoughts, new perspectives. Practice minimizing those old low-level beliefs.

Don't tire. Your life is worth it.

In Practice:

Challenge yourself to tell the whole story.

"I'm overwhelmed" is a headline. Practice telling the whole story. I've created my priorities. I have opportunities to simplify. I can be a better steward of my time. There are things I can drop and/or delegate.

"I can't do this" is a headline. Practice telling the whole story. I am doing it, I just don't like it. This is a season, and there is no season that lasts forever. This season has brought forth seeds of desire that I am responsible for cultivating. There are opportunities that have been and will be brought forth from this difficulty.

Refuse to be a headline reader! Anchor yourself to possibility, to your goals, to your hopes, and to your next chapters.

PUSHING OR PULLING

One of my friends shared with me a tool that she and her husband use in their marriage. When they find themselves arguing with each other, or even just being distant, one of them will ask the other, *"Are you pushing or pulling?"*

In what you're doing, saying, or feeling, are you pulling us together or are you pushing us apart?

I can think of so many times when although I desired closeness or connection, I pushed instead of pulled. I can't tell you how many times I've wanted to connect with Chris and pulled further away when he seemed to be more interested in a television show or a game on his phone. I pushed even though my desired outcome required pulling. When I wanted closeness, I behaved in a way that made it impossible.

We do this with people, but we also do this with ourselves.

Have you ever been frustrated with your health or your

weight and used that frustration to justify overindulging? That's pushing, not pulling.

Have you ever been angry at a friend for not reaching out, and so when they do finally call, you don't answer?

In my marriage, in my thoughts, and in my daily choices I've started asking myself: are you fighting against what you should be fighting for?

The key to this question being effective is your willingness to pause and ask it instead of barreling forward with your patterned behavior. The next critical step is being willing to answer honestly.

I ask myself that question when I get frustrated with Chris or when we're arguing. As we have this conversation, are we fighting against what we should be fighting for? Are we pushing or pulling?

I ask myself this when I'm talking myself out of a workout. Have you ever had one of those days where you reason with yourself, *"I don't feel like it. I have so many other things to do. I'll do it tomorrow"*? Are you fighting against what you should be fighting for?

Asking myself that question in those moments often guides

me to, *"What would it look like to fight for this instead of against it?"*

What would it look like to fight for a workout instead of against it?

What would it look like for me to fight for connection with Chris instead of against it?

What would it look like to fight for my health and happiness instead of against it?

Are you pushing or pulling?

Are you fighting against what you should be fighting for?

What would it look like to fight for what you're fighting against?

These questions are incredibly powerful when the moments feel hardest. These are the times when I've noticed the greatest tendency to push instead of pull, to fight against instead of fighting for. These questions have the most impact in the moments when I'm telling myself I don't care, it doesn't matter, or I don't want to do the work.

These are trench tools, not mountaintop tools.

I've fought against people who hurt me instead of fighting for the relationship.

I've fought against the things that help me heal like eating well, meditating, and moving instead of fighting for them.

I've pushed away from closeness and connection instead of pulling people closer.

When you recognize that you're fighting against what you want to be fighting for, that's the beginning of change. That's your doorway to a new pattern.

There's a Stephen Covey quote that I decided to journal about this morning. It says, *"Live out of your imagination, not your history."*

How different life would be if we lived from a place of what is possible instead of from a place of our past.

As I started to journal about what this would look like for me, as I wrote about what would change, I realized the biggest opportunity this quote held for me. What if I interacted with friends and family based on what is possible instead of based on their past? I'll be honest—especially as it relates to the people I'm closest to—I tend to operate based on what I expect from them, which is entirely based on the past. How much better could I make my relationships if

I stopped emphasizing the past and started to create the true potential?

What if my own choices were all based on what is possible—for my life, my work, my health, my relationships—instead of on my past or my history? I imagine everything would change. My goals would change, my attitude would change, my perspective would change, my mood would change.

Differentiating between goals and commitments reminds me to also differentiate between feelings and decisions. I've had to practice this thousands of times in this impossible season.

Feelings fluctuate. Decisions are always yours and do not hinge on your feelings, even if you tell yourself they do. You can make a strong decision regardless of your emotional weather.

I challenge you today to do all things and have all conversations from a place of what is possible instead of from a place of expectations derived from your past.

In Practice:

Create a habit of asking the questions. Enlist your partner, your kids, or a friend to use these questions with you.

Promise yourself that before skipping a workout or picking a fight, you'll run through these questions and give them the time and headspace they deserve.

Pro tip: Ask them out loud, put them in writing, or turn them into a conversation with someone you trust.

Commit to never stop at *"I don't know"* or give up with *"I don't care."* Choose to be the kind of person who sees those responses as starting points, not stopping points.

DATA OVER DRAMA

About eight weeks after Dagny was born, I stepped on the bathroom scale for the first time in about a year. The number looking up at me was a lot higher than I wanted it to be. Though I was far from psyched about the number, I have to say I was proud of my lack of drama. My body doesn't lie, after all. Objectively, I was bigger than I had been when I weighed less.

I had carried a baby for ten months. I delivered her only two months ago. I had a C-section. I hadn't been working out like I used to or even eating as well as I did when I weighed less. I knew those things even without knowing the number. The number reflected the facts.

I thought about how dramatic I used to be about the number on the scale, as though I had no idea of my habits.

Years ago, seeing the number on the scale could trigger me to create a total nightmare of dramatic thoughts. *OMG. I can't believe it. I've gained so much weight.* Disgust. Shame. Frustration. Anger. Regret.

Fortunately, I've become a better thinker. On this particular day, though I didn't like it and certainly would prefer a lower number, data merely reflected fact.

I didn't like it, and I could change it. There are steps I could take on any given day or in any given moment to change it.

Data driven, not drama driven. That's how I want to be, therefore that's how I have to practice being.

Once you start actively looking for them, you'll be shocked by how many opportunities life will give you to practice being data driven, not drama driven.

The very same day that I checked my weight for the first time after Dagny was born, I took an ovulation predictor test. It was positive. Great! Except it was the eighth consecutive day of a positive reading for ovulation, which I knew was not normal. As I looked at the positive result flashing on the screen of the test stick, I unconsciously opted for drama driven.

What's wrong? Something is wrong. I can't get pregnant again if I don't have a normal cycle. And the longer it is before my period starts, the longer it is until I ovulate. What if my cycle never returns to normal? What if I can't have any more kids?

Drama. Recognizing its familiar feeling, I reminded myself that I want to be data driven, not drama driven.

The first cycle after pregnancy is often usual. It can take time for your body to come back "online" after surgery, pregnancy, or emotional trauma, and I've had all three!

I challenged myself to focus on what parts of the process I could influence. This is not entirely outside of my control. There are things I can do to work with my body, and not against it, to stabilize my hormones and normalize my cycle.

Drink water

Eat lots of veggies

Minimize sugar and starch

Eat healthy fats

Walk

Meditate

Lift weights

Get enough sleep

We know it...drama is draining.

Imagine someone on your team at work always responds dramatically, no matter the situation. Every time a problem arises at the office, they blame themselves, call themselves stupid, and run to the bathroom in hysterics.

They wouldn't be on your team long, would they? That way of operating is not productive; it's immature and exhausting.

Well, I am the most valuable player on *my own* team. You are the most valuable player on *your own* team. We get to choose to hold ourselves to standards of objectivity, creativity, and a solution focus.

As I wrote these words, I got *another* chance to practice being data driven and not dramatic. It was crunch time before baby would arrive, so I eagerly worked on these pages. I planned for a super productive morning of writing and editing. Within thirty minutes of sitting down to write, there were eight cars in the driveway and twelve people in and around the house. The cleaning ladies were here. The pool company came two months early to dig and build our pool. Our construction project manager and his crew showed up to finish punch list items that should have been addressed months earlier.

Honestly, I wanted to cry. How am I supposed to concentrate with all of this going on? When I wrote *Chasing Cupcakes*, I'd simply go to the library or a coffee shop to escape the distractions of home, but with COVID-19, those strategies aren't options for this book. I started to think dramatically. *Can I just catch a break? I'll never get this done! I can't work like this!*

Like before, I recognized what drama feels like and chose to shift to data.

It's 9 a.m. The cleaning ladies will be gone in an hour. The construction crew will be gone by noon. I can put in headphones to block out the pool crew outside. There's plenty of other tasks I can do if I want to write later when it's more quiet. Most importantly, these people are here because I paid them to be. This isn't happening to me. I can ask every one of them to leave if I need or choose to. But I don't choose to, so conserve energy and stop complaining.

I reminded myself how valuable it is to get better at working with distractions. One of the best shifts I ever made in my personal development was embracing distractions during my meditation sessions. When I first started meditating, I'd get so irritated if someone came to the door or Chris interrupted my session. Sometime later, I heard someone suggest that we consider those moments to be part of our meditation session. Stay relaxed. Welcome them. This is life. Since then, my meditation practice has deepened dramatically and there's no longer a sense that I need peace and quiet to meditate.

I know for sure that writing, editing, and creating with distractions would bring similar benefits and resilience. With that perspective, I'm no longer annoyed but grateful for the opportunity to practice an important improvement.

Choose data, not drama.

In Practice:

Where do you often respond dramatically? Consider your health, lifestyle choices, finances, friendships, romantic relationships, family relationships, business, career, and any other relevant area of your life.

Where does drama show up most often in your life or in your thoughts or relationships?

As you experience drama, frustration, or unwanted emotion, ask yourself: in this situation, what would it look like to practice being data driven instead of drama driven?

What's the difference between the data and the drama?

Practice separating between what is happening and how you feel about what is happening.

Practice focusing on what you can do instead of what you can't or think you can't do.

EVIDENCE IS EVERYWHERE

Ever since we bought the old farmhouse property we now live on, Chris and I have wanted chickens and goats. We got chickens shortly after moving in, and we finally got baby goats a couple months after Dagny died.

We first brought home two adorable baby goats, and less than a week later, Chris told me we were getting three more! There were apparently three goats who needed to be rescued, so Chris and his big heart took them in.

The littlest of the new three was named Oliver. He had been abandoned by his mom and needed to be bottle-fed when we first got him. I loved him immediately. He was the runt and a cuddler with a huge personality.

One day, we noticed that Oliver had diarrhea. Being fairly new to goat ownership, we took the conservative approach and had the veterinarian come out to our house. She assured us that he was fine and left us with some probiotic drops for him.

Despite her assurances, I felt nervous. Doctors told us repeatedly that Dagny was healthy, and then we lost her so quickly. I likely projected that experience onto this precious little goat of ours. Nevertheless, I made Chris go down to check on him multiple times during the night. Everything was fine. The next morning, as Chris and I ate breakfast, I repeated my worry about Oliver, and Chris just rolled his eyes, his intolerance for my anxiety growing stronger. He assured me that Oliver was completely okay.

Minutes later, Chris went down to feed the goats and open up the chicken coop, as he did every morning.

When he came back up to the house, I immediately knew from the look on his face that something was wrong. Before he was even through the door I asked, *"What?"*

Somberly, he replied, *"Oliver."*

"Is he dead?!"

"Yes. It just happened. Maybe only a couple minutes before I went down."

I fell to pieces. I blamed myself. I blamed Chris. I blamed the vet.

A few hours later, I texted my friend who also has farm animals. I told her it felt like this situation paralleled what happened to Dagny in a most unwelcome way. Everything was fine, until it wasn't. I told her it made me feel like we aren't capable of caring for things. We couldn't save Dagny and we couldn't save Oliver.

The combination of Oliver's death and my perspective on it made for a terrible day.

As the hours went on, I continued to convince myself that this was my fault and that I clearly couldn't care for things. But then, in a very timely moment of emotional sobriety, I realized that while there was evidence for the story I told myself, there was even more evidence for a *different* story.

Evidence showed me that Oliver was sick when he got here and that was likely why his mother abandoned him. Evidence showed that we cared for him well. We bottle-fed him. We got him veterinary care. We showed him love. We rescued him.

Similarly, evidence showed that we cared well for Dagny, for our chickens, for our dog, for our other goats, for ourselves, and for each other.

You can find evidence for just about anything, but often, we settle on the evidence that supports the story we want to tell, whether it's good or bad.

We pick the set of data that supports our story and ignore the rest. That's a slippery slope and a dangerous way to live!

Your life is not about your circumstances. It's about your beliefs. Your beliefs determine how you see things and what you do about your circumstances.

Your beliefs determine the risks or steps you take and don't take. Your beliefs shape how you feel and behave.

The limit of your potential is your belief. Your beliefs set your expectations.

When my beliefs about myself are based on past behaviors, I repeat past behaviors because that's the expectation I've set.

As I see it, there are a few ways to go to optimize this:

First, stop endorsing and rehearsing the story of low-level belief.

Enough with the *"I just get so distracted"* and *"I'm really great at starting things but not so great at finishing them."* You will meet your own expectations. Refuse to rehearse that story.

Beyond that, you get to start creating evidence for the new story.

It can be small and simple at first. You started emptying the dishwasher and you finished. Look, you now have existing evidence of a new story: you finish what you start. Finish the workout strong. Now you have evidence that you *don't* always drift. You *can* finish strong. Make the end of your day the strongest part of your day. Now, do it again.

Evidence created. Evidence is everywhere. Look for it. Create it.

Your excuses and stories can keep you from expanding.

"I don't know" keeps you from expanding your mind.

"I'm afraid to fail" keeps you from experiencing success.

"I don't have time" keeps you from becoming more efficient.

"I'm too tired" keeps you from developing self-trust.

"He made me mad" keeps you from taking responsibility.

"It won't make a difference" keeps you from excellence.

I want you to take a minute today and ask yourself:

How is my excuse keeping me from expanding? Am I limiting myself by the evidence I'm focusing on?

You don't have to overcome all your excuses today, but pick one and decide that it doesn't get a vote today.

Overwhelmed doesn't get a vote.

Stressed doesn't get a vote.

Scared doesn't get a vote.

Say to yourself, *"I will not let my tried and tired excuses keep me from expanding any longer."*

There is evidence for everything.

In Practice:

Create a habit of asking yourself, *"What other evidence is there?"*

What other case could you make here?

What beliefs do you have about this?

What other beliefs are possible?

How might somcone else see or believe in this situation?

What evidence can you create for the belief you want to have?

DEFEATED OR DISTRACTED?

Sometimes we're only defeated because we're distracted.

Sometimes we're *not* defeated, we're just distracted.

Yesterday, I talked on the phone with a potential client, and she was frustrated. I listened to her share all the ways she is holding herself back and all the things she has committed to but isn't consistently following through on.

She sounded defeated, but it was clear to me; she was distracted. She was distracted by her past and the way things have been. She was distracted by a focus on what hasn't worked. She was so distracted by the problem that she couldn't see the solution. She wasn't looking that way.

Where you feel defeated, are you actually just distracted?

Are you distracted by time spent watching TV or following social media?

Are you distracted by your focus on how things have been or the missteps of yesterday?

Are you distracted by your own thoughts about temptation?

Are you distracted by your fears or insecurities?

During one of my long walks on the canal, I realized just how much my fears distracted me. I simply couldn't *see* hope or confidence. I focused on the fears and didn't look in the direction of my faith. I gave my energy to the obstacle and not to the way. I focused on the problem and not the solution.

In those moments, return again to what you want.

Return again to who you want to be.

Turn away from what you *don't* want and set your eyes on what you *do* want.

If you see fear, look again.

If you see doubt, look again.

If all you see is loss, look again.

I don't think you're defeated. I think you might be distracted. You don't need to fight, you need to focus.

Author and thought leader Cal Newport says that focus is the new IQ.

More often than not, you don't need to know more. You don't need to learn more. You don't need to fight harder. You need to focus.

In this season of my life, I need to focus on what I want and what I can do each day to bring it into existence.

I don't need to fight against my fears or fight against my grief. I need to focus on what I want and what I'm able and willing to do each day to create or influence it. This is another way of stating my mantra, *"The grief can ride with me, but it cannot drive."*

I choose to focus on what will contribute to my healing today.

I choose to focus on taking great care of myself.

I choose to focus on possibility and abundance.

I choose to focus on the people and things that are here for me instead of fighting against those that aren't.

You don't need to fight, you need to focus.

You don't need to fight what has happened to you.

You don't need to fight your feelings.

You don't need to fight other people and how they have or haven't responded to you or your circumstances.

You don't need to fight your past or even your own thoughts.

You need to focus.

Not long ago, I saw a quote from Akese Stylelines on Instagram that said, *"Use the weekend to build the life you want instead of trying to escape the life you have."*

How's that for a mic drop?

How many times do we get distracted by all the things we use to escape—television, social media, food, alcohol, or spending money? Don't fight the life you have; create the life you want.

I talk to so many clients who are fighting. They're frustrated, disappointed, down, discouraged—they're fighting their fears, their past, and their insecurities or doubts instead of focusing on what they want and what they can do about it.

Don't fight it. You don't have to like it, but things are the way they are right now.

Use your energy in focusing on what you can do now to create a change.

You don't need to fight, you need to focus.

You're not defeated, you're distracted.

In Practice:

In what area of your life do you feel defeated or doubtful?

In that area, what do you focus on most? What do you think about, fixate on, replay, or worry about most often?

Are these things distractions?

What do you need to focus on to create results?

What can you do today to bring about your desired outcomes?

EXCITED AND ALIVE

I am perpetually saving quotes and concepts that inspire me, make me think, or that strike me as a great idea to implement. I've gotten in the habit of putting them in my calendar as recurring meetings so I'm sure to see them multiple times. Without that practice, I'm likely to forget them as quickly as I stumbled upon them. I've been doing this for so long that most days of the year have multiple quotes or ideas saved in my calendar.

Not long after Dagny died, I clicked to open a quote that I saved as a meeting in my calendar.

"Whatever it is that makes you feel excited and alive, that clears the path for more of what you feel passionate about, that helps you feel connected to the charm of navigating endless twists and turns within the labyrinth of your own imagination—allow it to be part of your day...allow it to be part of your life."

—CARRIE CIULA

Unlike whatever day I found it and chose to save it, it didn't resonate with me *at all* on this day. It felt so far from my present state of mind that I couldn't even fathom having ever connected to it.

As I read it, my mind went blank: I couldn't imagine something making me feel excited or alive. At best, I could relate to longing, but not excitement or aliveness. I longed for a redo. I longed to have Dagny back. I longed to feel surrounded by my family like I had seen and cherished when other family members had passed. I longed for a very different life, but now, I was stumped by the notion of making room in my day for things that made me feel excited and alive.

If you feel stumped or stuck as you consider this quote, you're not alone. However, that is where we *start*. It's *not* where we stop. Sometimes we're more committed to saying we don't get it or it doesn't apply than we are to figuring it out and applying it.

This is the work of becoming a better thinker.

Reminding myself that the disconnect I felt was in fact a starting point, I looked for some other part of the quote I might connect with. *Twists and turns within the labyrinth of my imagination...*

I've created those twists and turns in my imagination, and I've regularly entered that labyrinth of worry, doubt, and fear. Surely that's not what the quote means to reference, but it was a starting point of connection. In fact, just the evening before I had experienced those twists and turns purely in my mind.

We have a two-year-old charcoal Labrador retriever named Rumi. In an attempt to keep him occupied until Chris came home, I had given him one of those rubber KONG balls filled with treats.

From the kitchen island where I sat working, I could hear him aggressively chewing the rubber toy. Randomly I thought, *"I wonder if Rumi could get so determined to extract the treats that he swallows the whole toy..."*

Then I entered the twists and turns of my imagination...

> *He'd surely choke. There's no way I'd get him to the vet on time. In fact, I probably couldn't get him to the car on my own. He's big, awkward, and over 130 pounds!*

> *I could try to give him the Heimlich, but does that even work on dogs? What are you supposed to do if a dog chokes?*

> *Would I call Chris? He couldn't help over the phone. Oh God, I couldn't handle it if I killed Rumi with a treat!*

The labyrinth of our imagination doesn't work just one way, even if we've only been *using* it one way. We can create twists and turns from worry and doubt just as we can create twists and turns from possibility and potential.

Remembering how I had used my imagination for worry and dread, I reminded myself that I have the same creative power to use it to dream of great things that could be possible. You have that same creative power.

I reminded myself that *"what if"* works both ways.

Before you head into a big meeting with your boss...

Oh my gosh, what if I get fired?

How long would my savings last?

What would I do if they ran out?

How long before a bank will foreclose on a house?

Would my parents let me move in with them at my age?

You can take the same starting point and create a wildly different trajectory inside the labyrinth of your imagination.

What if I get a raise?

What if I can share this important idea I have?

What if we make a great connection and I impress her?

What if this is my perfect opportunity to make some suggestions and create a new role for myself?

The labyrinth of your imagination isn't just a dark, negative, scary place. It might just be that you've exercised that part more than the positive, exciting place.

I'm not saying we have to only consider the positive possibilities, but at a minimum, we can explore both. We *should* explore both. We should never limit ourselves to only the possible negative or frightening outcomes.

Already, I connected to the quote.

I reminded myself that when I'm considering the possibilities that we might not have the huge family we want, I need to also entertain that we might! I need to indulge the positive possibilities as much as, and ideally more than, the potentially negative ones.

Chris and I have been told countless times that the divorce rate for couples who lose a child is over 80 percent. When I consider that our loss and our different experiences of it might destroy our marriage, I need to spend as much energy and effort, ideally more, considering and investing in the possibility that it could make us stronger and fortify a bond we wouldn't have otherwise had!

I returned to the quote with this newfound connection to see how else I might connect with it.

"Whatever it is that makes you feel excited and alive, that clears the path for more of what you feel passionate about, that helps you feel connected to the charm of navigating endless twists and turns within the labyrinth of your own imagination—allow it to be part of your day...allow it to be part of your life."

What do I feel passionate about? At the moment? Nothing.

Okay, that's where I start, not where I stop.

What do I *want* to feel passionate about? What have I felt passionate about in the past? Who are some passionate people I admire, and what do they appear to be passionate about? Is there another word, other than passionate, that's similar and more relatable? Want. What do I want? What do I wish I had more of in my life? What *would* get me excited, if I knew it was for me?

Ah, that last one did it for me. I could connect to that question.

What *would* get me excited, if I knew it was for me?

I would get excited if I knew my best-case scenario life was for me. From there, I had to get specific. What's my best-case scenario life?

I make a full-time living as a writer and podcaster. My books are in high demand, and I'm working ten hours per week. We have six or seven children, and our house is full of love, laughter, and positive energy. We have built a beautiful barn on our property that includes a full gym for me and a massive indoor jungle gym for the kids. Most of our days are spent playing, gardening, swimming in the pool, and enjoying each other. Chris and I are best friends, and we adore each other and the life we've created.

Even though I still might not connect to the words "excited and alive," I've connected with the quote and shifted my energy in a matter of minutes.

You might be wondering why I think it's important to do the work to connect with a quote I've saved. Connecting with it helps me put it into action. I could have just read it, not related, and moved on. However, doing the work to create connection opens the door for me to consider how I might put it into action in my life.

In this case, it helped me start to dream. It reminded me to make that dreaming a practice, even if I'm hurting. Maybe even especially if I'm hurting.

It's okay if you don't have a passion. Still, start dreaming. Ask other people about their dreams.

Stand guard against the negativity and the doubt. Yes, you can make a case for why anything is hard or unlikely, but that's not why you're doing this.

Dreaming is a muscle most of us have to build. No one is judging your thoughts. If you're judging them, that's okay. You can dream and judge at the same time. The judging or doubt won't keep you from dreaming unless you decide to stop.

In Practice:

Take yourself through the same process and inquiry with the Carrie Ciula quote as I shared in this chapter.

Where can your imagination take you that is positive?

Where can your imagination take you that is hopeful?

Where can your imagination take you that is ideal?

Where can your imagination take you that excites you?

What parts of those visions do you influence? How do you influence them? Is there something you're able and willing to do today to influence them?

Notice when you're using your imagination for doubt, dread, fear, or worst-case scenarios. In those moments, don't judge yourself for the use of your imagination, but challenge yourself to use your imagination in equal measure to explore the best-case scenario!

FOCUS BEFORE FEELING

One of the most empowering things I tell myself is that every-thing is a *focus* before it's a *feeling*. Stress is a focus before it's a feeling. Overwhelm is a focus before it's a feeling.

Just the other day, I felt overwhelmed by my to-do list. I cre-ated a list of the things I want to complete before baby boy makes his arrival. The list was *long*. I wanted to get three months ahead on podcasts. I wanted to finish writing and editing this book. I wanted to officially change my name and do everything that comes along with that. There were easily fifty things on the list, some quick to knock out and others that would take weeks or months. As I focused on *all* the things, I started to feel stressed and overwhelmed.

My overwhelm was a focus before it was a feeling. Instead of focusing on what I would do next, I focused on *all* the things. In a single moment, I focused on months of to-dos.

It's always a focus first.

I see this play out in my marriage on a regular basis. If I focus on the fact that Chris didn't hang up the shirts I asked him to yesterday, I start to feel annoyed. If I focus on the fact that he left his milk glass in the sink again, I start to feel irritated. If I focus on him not wanting to talk about Dagny, I feel sad. It's a focus before it's a feeling.

When I focus on the last time Chris made me laugh, I feel lighthearted or grateful.

When I focus on how he came upstairs last night just to rub my feet, I feel appreciative.

When I focus on our recent breakfast date when we talked easily about fond childhood memories, I feel connected.

It's always a focus before it's a feeling. It's empowering to realize that the feeling can't be generated without there first being a focus.

You will feel overwhelmed only after you focus on the twenty things on your to-do list. You will feel overwhelmed only after you focus on the fact that there are just ninety minutes left to finish your project. You will feel angry only after you focus on what that person did or said, didn't say or didn't do.

Because we can change our focus, we can also change our feelings.

Remember the story I shared about imagining Rumi choking on the toy? The focus came before the feeling. I focused on the possibility of him choking and being unable to save him before I started feeling anxious and afraid.

I'm not sharing this with you to tell you that feeling overwhelmed, annoyed, or angry is bad, just like feeling hopeful or empowered isn't better. I simply want you to remind yourself that we have the power to shift how we feel by shifting our focus.

I have had countless opportunities to practice this in my grief. I have an immediate family member who I reached out to the day Dagny died. I had been texting him for prayers, and within an hour or two of her death, I let him know that she passed. He did not call me for more than four months after that. He never asked how I was. He never asked what he could do. He didn't call to check in or to offer support or see if we needed help. He called four months later only because it was my birthday.

When I focus on it, it makes me mad. When I focus on it, it makes me sad. The focus always comes before the feeling.

Sometimes, the thoughts come into my mind spontaneously. Sometimes someone in my life brings it up and into my focus. I hate feeling that hurt and angry, especially during such a sensitive time in my life. I get to remind myself that it's only a feeling because of my focus. I'm not wrong for feeling that way, and I certainly don't have to change my focus. It's perfectly fine if I want to marinate in those feelings. But I don't have to. I can change my focus.

Recently, I worked with a client who was so fired up to get more consistent with her exercise routine. She felt that was her key to motivation, mindset, and ultimately weight loss. Right out of the gate, she injured her hand such that she couldn't do her beloved Pilates routine without modifications. Days later, she injured her foot. Not surprisingly, she was bummed. When she focused on what she couldn't do, she felt defeated. When she adjusted her focus to the hundreds of things she still *could* do, she felt entirely differently.

If you want to change how you feel, change your focus.

Focus on gratitude, and it will change how you feel.

Focus on your blessings, and it will change how you feel.

Focus on what you've done right, and it will change how you feel.

Focus on what others have done right, and it will change how you can feel.

In Practice:

This is a practice you can employ anytime, and I encourage you to not limit your practice to when you're upset. I've found it to be easier to practice when I'm *not* in a negative mood state.

Let's say you observe that you're feeling in control. You have a solid plan for your day or week, and you feel empowered as you focus on the plan. Decide to intentionally shift your focus to something that elicits feelings of gratitude. Change your focus to someone who did something thoughtful for you or focus on all your body has done for you in the last twenty-four hours.

Recall, in maximum detail, the last time you laughed hysterically. Observe how changing your focus changed how you feel.

Gradually, look for opportunities to practice in moments where you want to change your feeling.

Overwhelm is a great place to get in easy practice. Instead of focusing on all the things you "need" to do, focus on all the things other people in your life are responsible for doing that help you. Maybe you focus on a coworker who changed the ink in the printer, or your son who carried the trash out, or the plumber who fixed your garbage disposal. Thank goodness for them! Or identify how many of the things on your list are "optional"—nothing bad will happen if they don't get done, you just want them done. Watch the pressure melt away and the feeling shift as you realize this original feeling is self-imposed. Choose to focus on what you need to do now and remove your focus from all the things you want to do in the next day or week.

Look for opportunities to practice when you're agitated, sad, or lonely.

It's always a focus before it's a feeling!

DRAMA-FREE RE-ENGAGEMENT

If I had a magic wand and could grant all of us just one superpower, it very well might be the ability to re-engage in any moment without drama.

I can't tell you how many times I've viewed a setback as a problem and become fifty shades of upset or stressed about it. A month or two after Dagny died, I wanted to prioritize my health. My cortisol levels were through the roof. Stress, anxiety, and depression were exhausting me, and I knew they could keep us from our goal of conceiving another child.

There were some basic adjustments I knew I needed to make like minimizing processed foods, limiting sugar and starch, and maximizing nutrient density. I knew what to do and I knew what *not* to do, but sometimes I chose a different path. One day I drove to a local bakery and bought four cupcakes. I picked two flavors for Chris and two for myself, and I figured we'd snack on them throughout the week. I ate all four while driving home. I don't think I even tasted them, I just shoveled them in my mouth.

I knew it wasn't good for my stress hormones.

I knew it wasn't good for my anxiety and depression.

I knew it wouldn't support my goal of getting pregnant and being fertile for many years to come.

I did it anyway.

As I walked into the house with crumbs covering my shirt, I wondered, *"What is wrong with me? I want to be healthy and have a large family more than I want cupcakes! I can't believe I just mindlessly stuffed myself with sugar! What the hell?!"*

It's not the first time I've beat myself up for a choice or for my inconsistency and excuses. Hundreds, if not thousands, of times, I've replayed in my mind the choice I shouldn't have made or the commitment I didn't follow through on (again).

I talk to people every day who have the same pattern and create drama over a choice that is already behind them. They get mad at themselves, disappointed in their failure to follow through, or angry about their lack of results.

Here's what I know:

Success isn't a function of flawless performance or a perfectly executed plan.

Success is a function of how you *respond* to setback or struggle.

You will screw up.

You will make choices you wish you hadn't made.

You will let yourself down.

You will let others down.

You will drift, disengage, and make excuses.

You'll lose money.

You'll gain weight.

You'll take the wrong path.

Where you end up depends not on what you just did but on *what you do next*.

It's what happens *after* a moment of struggle that determines your success.

Do you create a *"Screw it, I blew it"* story?

Do you get pissed off or down on yourself?

Do you give away your energy and attention to the past and the problem?

Or do you choose to *re-engage in the present moment without drama*?

Our goal isn't to avoid struggles and setbacks.

Our goal is to improve how we respond to them.

How do you respond to the days, weeks, or months when you drift, disengage, or lose focus? You have a choice. You can stay in the drama and beat yourself up, or you can get back in the game.

As with most of the tools we've talked about so far, life is going to generously give you plenty of chances to practice.

I practice with food.

I practice with work challenges.

I practice in my marriage.

I practice with my thoughts.

Recently, I needed to get some old tax records from Chris from before we were married. Turns out, he had done a terrible job of keeping records and, quite frankly, it irritated me in a big way.

I started lecturing him about the importance of keeping good financial records and how it costs us money if he doesn't. I even told him to grow up and be responsible. Understandably, he got defensive.

Quickly, I acknowledged that I was being a bitch and didn't like myself for it. It's what comes *next* that matters most. I could continue to chastise him. I could ignore and avoid it. Or I could make a great choice. Success isn't about avoiding moments of struggle. It's about improving how we respond to them.

I apologized. I told him he impressed me with how far his money management has come in the last few years. I explained why it was so important to me, and I gave him a hug.

We're both going to have moments where we don't show up as our best, as a couple and individually. In these moments, we get to practice re-engaging in the present moment without drama. Without judgment. Without negativity or criticism. We get to practice getting right to the next best choice.

The week of Thanksgiving, I ate a *lot*. I had one thousand rationalizations for why each choice was *"fine."* I told myself it was fine because I wasn't in a season of weight loss as I have been on so many other holidays. I rationalized it because I was pregnant, because I didn't care, because I was grieving, and because it was insanely hard to navigate the first holidays without Dagny. I rationalized it because it looked good and tasted good. There was no shortage of rationalizations.

Predictably, a few days after Thanksgiving I felt like absolute garbage. I felt moody, tired, bloated, and generally down.

Here was yet another chance to practice drama-free re-engagement. I reminded myself that success is not about being flawless. I'm not screwed because I overate for a few days. I didn't do anything wrong. There's not even a problem.

My success comes from how I *respond* to these moments of feeling down or not keeping the commitments I've made.

Will I hang my head in shame? No.

Will I step into the *"Screw it, I blew it"* mode and make mac and cheese? No.

I'll practice drama-free re-engagement.

I'll make a breakfast smoothie with lots of protein and healthy fats. I'll go for a walk. Lift some weights. Drink lots of water and stay away from the cookies, cupcakes, and pie.

I've used this countless times while writing and editing this book. There have been days when I didn't complete the amount of work I committed to, and it's easy to create the narrative that I'm behind and can't catch up. But successful people keep moving.

I don't need to debate whether I can or can't catch up; I need to put my head down and get back to work.

Having a successful book isn't a function of perfect work ethic and admirable consistency. Having a successful book hinges on how I respond to the days and moments where I don't do the work, I don't show up, or I don't put my best foot forward.

I have a choice and so do you, every time.

Hard times may take us out of the game for a bit. That's okay. You aren't bad, you aren't wrong, you aren't screwed. Success is not out of reach for you because of the choices that are behind you. Success is about what you do with the choices that are in front of you!

Hard times can compete for your focus. They'll often shift your priorities. That's okay.

When you're ready, re-engage without drama.

There's no merit to manufacturing drama and judgment around the disengagement. It happens. I'd argue that there's no one who has achieved anything who did so perfectly.

In my first book, *Chasing Cupcakes*, I write about this problem/solution cycle that includes four phases:

Sensing

Seeking

Settling

Solving

Sensing is all about how you feel about the problem or circumstance. You're in the sensing phase when your thoughts and words surround frustration, disappointment, or any way you feel about the situation.

You're in the seeking phase when you're looking for options, you're looking for information, or you're searching for possible solutions.

The settling phase is all about deciding. I'm going to re-engage. I'm going to do the work. Sometimes this phase acts like a trap of sorts, because we can confuse the commitment with the work. Deciding isn't the same thing as doing.

In the solving phase, you're taking action. You're actively creating the change you want to see or be. You're doing the work. You're off the sidelines and in the game.

That's the phase we want to get to: solving. We'll have to return to it again and again if we want to make progress.

When people act like they're screwed or like they've created some problem because a work project distracted them from a weight loss goal or an injury got in the way of their fitness goal...I have to ask them, *"Did you have the expectation that nothing would get in your way and it would be a straight shot from where you started to where you want to go?"*

For many of them, that *was* the expectation. Personally, I think that perspective is inexperienced, immature, or both.

As I paid off my debt, not one single month went according to plan. *I still got out of debt.* Things came up constantly. A blown tire, a medical bill, an unexpected trip to see family, or that time the dog ate through the wall and we had to have it repaired (true story).

My success in getting out of debt hinged on how I *responded* to those things.

Sure, like many people, I could have said, *"This is why we can never get ahead!"* But I didn't say that. I just re-engaged without drama. Sure, it might have added a few weeks or even a few months to our getting out of debt process, but it still felt entirely doable.

The same is true in business. There are setbacks and hurdles, big issues and small every single week.

Did I expect that building a business would be a flawless trajectory from the start to the fulfillment of my goals? No, I didn't. People have lied to me, stolen money, stolen content, and then some. My site has crashed, my server has crashed, and I've sent out broken links in the middle of a launch. I've had great ideas that went nowhere and bad ideas I stayed with for far too long. I've said the wrong thing, I've upset clients, and yet my success as a business owner hinges only on how I respond to those things.

My success has nothing to do with avoiding mistakes or problems.

The problems will be plentiful. Each time, practice drama-free re-engagement.

In Practice:

This is largely a practice of perspective. You can either see setbacks as problems, or you can see them as part of the process. You cannot progress without setback, struggle, or challenge. These aren't problems at all; they are milestones and normal parts of your process.

In what areas of your life do you need to practice this perspective shift?

In what areas of your life do you have evidence that you succeeded or made progress despite setbacks?

How can you improve your response to perceived failure, struggle, setback, or challenge?

How will you practice this today?

TOLERANCE FOR TENSION

My mom started CrossFit in her midsixties. Though she had been active throughout her adult life, walking, kayaking, and playing tennis, she didn't have much experience with weights or high intensity workouts. In fact, she had never even touched a barbell. Prior to CrossFit, her idea of lifting weights was using pink dumbbells and machines. I felt encouraged to hear she had joined CrossFit because I knew the presence of a good coach would help her get out of her comfort zone and lifting heavier weights.

The reality of those very light weights is that most of us won't see results with them because they don't provide enough of a stimulus. In some areas, including strength training, results are a function of stimulus and response. The greater the stimulus, the greater the response.

Muscle maintenance and muscle growth require time under tension.

For better or for worse, humans are generally the same way. If our trials are the five- or ten-pound kind (in dumbbell equivalent), we won't grow much. They simply don't provide enough of a stimulus.

Like our muscles, it's total tension, and time under tension, that determines how much we can grow.

The greater the stimulus, the greater the response.

That might make you groan. I know when I think about it, I don't love it. *Fantastic. Trials are required. And the bigger the trial, the bigger the potential for growth. Wonderful. Sounds like fun.*

It's *not* fun. However, as I look back, I can see how true it is. When I get a flat tire, it's frustrating and annoying, but it's essentially a "one-pound struggle." There's not a lot of total tension. There's not much time under tension. There's not much potential for growth. Sure, I want to use those tiny trials to practice becoming a better thinker, but in and of themselves, they won't take me very far.

Renovating my house is probably a ten- or fifteen-pound struggle. It's a lot more time under tension, a lot more total tension than the flat tire, and it's definitely helped me grow intellectually and emotionally.

Losing Dagny feels like a one-thousand-pound struggle. I don't think I can effectively quantify the total time under tension. The rest of my life? As much as I'd trade in the potential growth and maturation to have my daughter back, I can objectively say that the growth I've experienced in my perspective, in my patience, and in my ability to live fully and know what matters is immeasurable.

The greater the trial, the greater the potential for growth. I am not sharing that to encourage you, but to let you know that these things do serve a purpose, as unwanted as it may be.

If all you see is the time under tension, you won't see the potential for growth.

When you stand and evaluate your tension or your trouble, you're not wrong about what you see. It's hard, it's frustrating, devastating, isolating, and uncertain. It's all of those things. You're right. But that's not all there is.

If you only see the tension, you're probably missing a lot of the truth.

During my senior year in college, my stepdad died in a car accident. I'm not wrong when I look back on the situation and see the loss, the years under tension, and the ways it impacted our family. All of that is very true. It's just not the *only* truth. I also grew so much from the loss.

I grew up very quickly. It was the first unexpected loss of my life where you think someone will be home at seven and they simply never come home.

I can say the same about the end of my first marriage. There was more than loss. I grew in necessary and unexpected ways from that time under tension.

Whether you choose to see it or not, the same is true for you and the trials in your life.

The greater the total tension and the greater the time under tension, the greater your capacity for growth.

In Practice:

Begin to view moments or seasons of struggle as the emotional equivalent to strength training. You will quickly feel defeated if you see it as a burden or perceive that you are a victim of your circumstances.

This doesn't mean you have to like, appreciate, or desire your circumstances, but choose the perspective that in ways that may be seen and may be unseen, you are training your mental, emotional, cognitive, and psychological strength.

When you find that your attention is on the hardship, seek to find a moment or a sliver of appreciation in that hardship.

Estimate the weight equivalent of your challenge or hardship. Not only will this put things into perspective and help you avoid getting your feathers ruffled over "one-pound problems," but it will also help you more easily see the opportunity a larger challenge represents for your growth, resilience, and maturation.

WORK ETHIC

In his book *The Happiness Advantage,* Shawn Achor writes, *"Happiness isn't just a feeling; it's a work ethic."*

In the months after Dagny died, I remember talking about this quote with the Primal Potential Masters Club, and I struggled to connect with it. I couldn't relate to happiness at the time.

I turned to my go-to strategy that I've already shared with you—I looked for another part of the quote I *could* connect with and considered other ways I might apply or relate to the idea.

I started with the notion of work ethic. After considering what work ethic means to me, I looked it up in the dictionary.

Here's how the Merriam-Webster Dictionary defines it:

> *"A set of values centered on the importance of doing work and reflected especially in a desire or determination to work hard."*

Keeping in mind that specificity is a superpower, I wanted to dig deeper. I asked myself, *"Where do I feel like I demonstrate solid work ethic? Where do I have a determination, backed by action, to work hard?"*

I looked at my career. I have a solid work ethic there. Considering my career, what does a strong work ethic look like?

What are the things I do or don't do that reflect what I consider to be a solid work ethic?

> I work whether I feel like it or not.

> I put forth tremendous effort.

> I'm constantly learning how to do things better.

> I ask for feedback.

> There isn't much variation in how I show up day-to-day or week-to-week.

I have a similar work ethic with my finances.

> I monitor things closely.

> I put in a lot of effort.

I'm always trying to learn new things and expose myself to new ideas or approaches.

I routinely measure my results.

I set goals and take steps almost every day to make progress towards those goals.

From there, I returned to the notion of happiness. Given the clarity I now had on what work ethic looked like in other areas of my life, *do I apply a similar approach to happiness?*

At first thought...nope. I sure don't. I knew I would benefit most from more specificity, so I kept digging.

Do I work to create happiness every day? No.

Do I have clear action steps that would increase my happiness? No.

Do I put in a lot of effort to be happy? No.

Do I routinely measure my happiness? No.

Am I in a habit of learning about happiness or exploring new ways to feel happy? Nope.

Like many people, until this point I had thought of happiness a feeling. I hadn't thought of it or treated it as a work ethic. But I love this newer-to-me view.

Happiness *is* a work ethic. We have to apply ourselves regularly and with great effort.

As much as I loved the idea, I once again felt at a loss in terms of what might make me happy. I'm sure that in other seasons of my life I wouldn't have struggled as much with this concept, but in a time of grief, depression, anxiety, and uncertainty, I didn't even know where to start with happiness action steps.

Not knowing is where our work *begins*, not where our work *ends*.

I decided to start by considering the opposite.

What is making me unhappy? What is in my life that I don't enjoy or that contributes to feelings that are in conflict with happiness (stress, anxiety, worry, disdain)?

Maybe "happiness as a work ethic" can begin with removing or minimizing what makes me unhappy. Maybe progress towards increased happiness can begin by eliminating the barriers to happiness to whatever extent I can do so.

Friend, this isn't just about happiness. We can bring the same creative problem-solving to just about anything.

Mental peace isn't just a feeling; it's a work ethic.

Enthusiasm isn't just a feeling; it's a work ethic.

Passion isn't just a feeling; it's a work ethic.

Motivation isn't just a feeling; it's a work ethic.

Confidence isn't just a feeling; it's a work ethic.

Security isn't just a feeling; it's a work ethic.

This is a tool I relied on heavily during the first holiday season after Dagny died. I felt devastated. Of course, there is nothing wrong with feeling sad, but I didn't want to feel so sad all the time, and I knew intellectually that I could shift my feelings with some consistent effort.

When I looked at my disposition through the lens of the fact that happiness is a work ethic, I could clearly see why I felt so down. I hadn't done any work, and certainly not any hard work, to be happy. I hadn't been consistent, and I didn't have daily disciplines or action steps in place to create the feeling of happiness.

I started with the smallest available steps.

I decided to listen to Christmas music every day when I showered, cooked, cleaned, or drove. I could, and wanted to, implement this small daily discipline.

I added a short walk to my calendar for just ten minutes daily during lunch. Fresh air and sunshine lift my mood and are certainly part of that happiness work ethic I worked to build.

Remembering that it's a focus before it's a feeling, I made a list of things I could focus on that generate feelings of happiness.

Sometimes, I still felt sad, and that's okay. That's the thing about viewing a feeling as a work ethic. You do it whether you want to or not. You do it whether it's convenient or not. You do it whether you see results immediately or not.

That's where we all can start.

In Practice:

Take an inventory of feelings you don't want to marinate in (overwhelm, anger, resentment, doubt, etc.).

Identify the feeling you *do* want to have. For example, calm, acceptance, peace, confidence. For each of these, go through the process outlined in this chapter.

Start with a series of questions that will help inform and define your practice:

What does work ethic mean to you?

In what areas of your life do you have a solid work ethic?

What makes it a great work ethic? What are the things you do or don't do, the ways you operate, that create that solid work ethic?

Where do you feel like you don't have a great work ethic?

What would it look like if you did have a great work ethic in that area? What would be different?

What would it look like to apply that approach to some of these things you want to feel more consistently?

What's in it for you? How do you win if you make that change?

Where will you start?

When will you start?

What actions will you take?

How will you stay mindful of this as a consistent daily practice?

How will you monitor your results?

FADING IS FINE

Several years ago, after hearing rave reviews from a handful of highly successful individuals, I decided to get trained in the practice of Transcendental Meditation (TM).

TM isn't something you learn online or in a book. You sit with a TM trainer through a handful of individual or group sessions and learn directly from someone with years of experience. My trainings were in a small group setting, and I remember being grateful for a question asked by one of the gentlemen in my group because I was having an experience similar to his.

He said, "*I feel amazing after I meditate. I feel calm, focused, and energized. It's hard to explain how significant the improvement is. The problem is, it seems to wear off fast. I feel great for a bit, but after just an hour or so, the effect is gone and I'm back to feeling rushed, agitated, or anxious. Is there a way to make the effects last longer?*"

I have felt this myself, with regards to meditation but also so many other things! It's a common frustration I've heard from clients with regards to focus, clarity, consistency, and motivation.

In response, our instructor shared one of the famous teachings from Maharishi Mahesh Yogi. It goes something like this...

Once upon a time, a woman, yearning for a bright yellow cloth, decided to dye a white garment. She prepared the rich yellow color and allowed the white cloth to soak in it. After some time, she removed the garment from the dye, thrilled to see the rich yellow hue. She set it to dry in the sun.

Much to her dismay, when she went to retrieve the cloth the next day, most of the color had faded! It barely retained a slight yellow tint.

Determined, she decided to soak it in the dye once more. After a good soak, she set the garment to dry in the sun.

The following day, she felt disheartened again. The color faded as it dried! It retained a little more of the color than the day before, but it was still far from the bright yellow she hoped it would be.

She repeated the process again and again, the color retaining just a bit more of its richness with each repetition.

It took some time, but eventually the cloth remained the bright yellow she desired.

So it is with Transcendental Meditation and just about everything else in life. As a result of regular practice, the effect is maintained more and more. It's a cumulative process that requires consistency over time.

Maybe at first your hopeful perspective is only maintained for a few seconds. But with regular practice, these increments will get longer.

Maybe at first your openness to new perspectives only lasts for an hour. Fortunately, with time and repetition, it can become an engrained habit.

The only reason our results *aren't* maintained is if we don't practice consistently.

It's okay if your motivation fades. It will. It's normal. You are in control of the retention process.

It's okay if your focus fades. It will. It's normal. You are in control of the retention process.

It's okay if your patient parenting approach fades. It will. It's normal. You are in control of the retention process.

It's okay if your improved outlook fades. It will. It's normal. You are in control of the retention process.

With regular practice, *everything* is maintained more and more. We have to be active in the process. This isn't something that happens because we do something once or twice. It doesn't happen because we want it or we learn about it. We have control of our retention, but it requires our consistent participation and repetition.

In Practice:

How does this story apply in your life?

What frustrates you with its lack of lasting results?

What fades for you?

Where do you need more repetition?

What do you want to establish as a lasting pattern or habit?

What will you do about it today?

WHEN POSITIVITY FEELS PAINFUL

It feels awkward to share this, but I imagine many of you can relate. In the last year, I've felt very protective of my pain. I've been reluctant to express positive emotions around the many good things that have happened this year. Yes, we had a staggering number of low moments, but there were some very special moments, too. We got pregnant again. We expanded and fully renovated our second floor. We put in a pool, got goats, and even got married! I surprised Chris with a new truck, my grandmother turned one hundred, and Chris's brother got married.

Every one of those moments made me uncomfortable. Every one of them felt bittersweet. With each one, I thought of Dagny and how she should have been part of it.

I hesitated to display any outward happiness or excitement. If I'm being totally honest, I think I was afraid that if people saw me laugh or smile, if they heard me say that we had a fun night or a good weekend, they would think I was over the pain of Dagny's death. They might think I was okay when I felt I was not. Maybe I'd get less support when I felt I needed it. I invented this idea that people might think I was no longer mourning, and that made me terribly uncomfortable.

When people made comments like *"It's great to see you smile"* or *"You look like you're doing well,"* I found myself getting defensive. At times, I almost wished I could prove my pain even though I knew that wouldn't serve any purpose.

Upon noticing this tendency, I sought to understand it more completely. *Why did I care whether or not people appeared to realize my pain? What was the need I had underneath all the fears and assumptions? Was it true that someone thinking I'm doing well meant they assumed I felt no pain of loss? Did it matter? What did I really want? How could I go about getting what I wanted instead of making assumptions about what people might think or do?*

Why was I considering emotion and perception in such binary ways? Could I do a better job of verbalizing the complexity of my feelings? Would that help? Had I tried?

I didn't have all the answers, but there were a few things I knew for sure. I didn't want to get comfortable living in sadness. I didn't want to operate as though I could only feel, experience, or express one thing at a time. Life doesn't limit us in that way. At the same time, I longed for people close to me to see and support my pain.

Had I asked for support? Had I identified and communicated what kind of support I wanted and from whom?

These questions helped me see that I didn't want or need support from *everyone*. I didn't need or expect understanding from strangers on the internet or casual acquaintances. I made a list of people whose understanding really mattered to me.

Looking at the list, I began to identify what I needed to do to get clarity about my feelings. I started by verbalizing the emotional complexity.

I sat down with Chris and tried to give my feelings a voice. I explained how I felt protective of my pain. I described my resistance to feeling or displaying any positive emotions. I expressed my fear of being misunderstood or not supported. As I shared with him, I realized how many of my feelings and fears were based on assumption or an incomplete version of the truth. Intellectually, I knew that grief and depression weren't isolated feelings—it's never that simple. I lived in a limitation I hadn't recognized.

I could be grateful and also deeply mourning.

I could be excited and also sad.

Yet here I feared that expressing one side meant denying the other.

I'm sharing this with you as a reminder that we can allow for and embrace both. There's no limit to how many things you can feel or experience at once. Maybe clinging to one emotional state is your sign that you have an unmet need. Maybe you need to improve how and what you're communicating about your feelings.

Sad and stressful things will happen continuously throughout our lives, and I don't want any of us to fight more for our pain than we do for our happiness. I don't want any of us to protect our pain in a way that keeps everything else at bay, including true connection.

I didn't want to create a pattern of trying to prove my pain to people who hadn't experienced it and could never understand it.

If you're feeling protective of your past, of your pain, of your anger, or of your fear, I want you to know that I understand. I also want you to know that it's a miserable way to live and that you can break out of that pattern.

You don't have to deny your pain, your past, or your anger, but you don't have to limit yourself to it either.

Live in multitudes. Look for contrast. Invite opposites.

Instead of gripping blindly to a familiar feeling, consider what else there is to experience. Make space for more than what you're used to.

This is a practice I've committed to as we prepare to bring our son into the world. I want to savor and celebrate every moment with him. I also want to create space for and give a voice to the pain of loss and missing out it brings up. These feelings aren't in conflict or competition.

I understand that positivity can feel painful. Don't forget that it's a focus before it's a feeling. Don't deny the pain, but be willing to welcome new perspectives.

In Practice:

What does your emotional comfort zone look like?

Is there an emotional area of your life where you feel misunderstood? Whose understanding do you seek? How can you improve your communication around your feelings?

Where are you living in a perceived limitation or making assumptions about how others view you or interpret your behavior?

Practice verbalizing and acknowledging the spectrum of thought and emotion present in any situation or circumstance.

Seek to live in multitudes. You don't have to choose, and your emotions aren't in conflict or competition!

WHAT HAPPENS AT THE END

Endings can be so hard. They're often unwanted, uncertain, and sometimes even traumatic. Keep this in mind: whether you like it or not, want it or not, acknowledge it or not, **every single ending is also a new beginning.**

The end of Dagny's life on earth was the beginning of her eternal life in Heaven.

The end of Dagny's life was the beginning of my life as a mother who lost a child.

The end of Dagny's life was also the beginning of my clarity about what I want our family to be.

The end of Dagny's life was the beginning of a different kind of relationship with my husband.

Sometimes, we only allow ourselves to see the end. That was certainly true for me with Dagny. For months, I let myself see the end of what I thought life would be. The end of my dreams for her. The end of motherhood.

Maybe this is what you experienced when you lost a job. The end of the opportunity. The end of certainty. The end of that paycheck.

No matter what, the end of something is the beginning of something else.

The end of this book is a new beginning. It's the beginning of your life with a new set of tools and perspectives.

As you go forward, I want you to use these tools.

I challenge you to think of your experience with this book as having purchased a set of tools. Will you let them sit on a shelf, or will you look to see which one you can use as you navigate tough circumstances, countless choices, and challenging moments?

Maybe there's one tool or perspective that resonated with you more than others and you want to stay focused on that one for a while. Keep it with you daily. Journal about it. Meditate on it. Look for opportunities in your day to apply it.

Maybe there were several tools you feel you need in this season of life. Consider making an index card for each one. Review it daily, multiple times each day, and ask yourself where and how you can apply it on that day.

Either way, this marks both the end of a book and the beginning of your application of it. These tools, strategies, and perspectives are only valuable to the extent that you use them!

Lastly, I want you to remember that evolution is tough to see up close. As you look at your situation from your current vantage point, it's impossible to see all of it. You don't know what's ahead. Be open to the reality that the seed cracks open in the dark, unaware of the bright new life on the other side of fear and loss.

ACKNOWLEDGMENTS

Dagny and Roman: I love you.

To my husband, Chris: I wish the world could see and know your bravery and steadfastness in our darkest moments. Thank you for holding me up, holding it down, and being the light of hope in our home. We couldn't save Dagny, but maybe we saved each other.

To my mom: I will never forget your bold display of love and devotion as you stood by Dagny's side during her last hours. You are a true example of the strength of a mother.

To all of my family, friends, clients, readers, and listeners who stood by my side as I have navigated these trenches of grief: I am eternally grateful. We're only just beginning.

ABOUT THE AUTHOR

ELIZABETH BENTON is the #1 bestselling author of *Chasing Cupcakes* and *Change Makers Productivity & Fulfillment Journal*, creator of the 12 Weeks to Transformation Self-Study program, and a seven-figure entrepreneur. Her wildly popular podcast, *Primal Potential*, has been downloaded millions of times.

Today, Elizabeth continues to develop new ways of helping women everywhere create lasting change. Find her online at PrimalPotential.com.

Made in the USA
Monee, IL
26 October 2021